CATHOLIC STORIES
OF FAITH AND HOPE

CATHOLIC STORIES
OF
FAITH AND HOPE

HOW GOD BRINGS GOOD
OUT OF SUFFERING

Authored and Compiled by
Steven R. Hemler

TAN Books
Gastonia, North Carolina

Published with Ecclesiastical Permission

Catholic Stories of Faith and Hope: How God Brings Good Out of Suffering © 2021 Steven R. Hemler

Cover design by Caroline Green

Cover image: Christ walking on the waters, 19th century facsimile reproducing a mural mosaic, Sicily, 7th century. Photo © Leonard de Selva / Bridgeman Images

Library of Congress Control Number: 2020952506

ISBN: 978-1-5051-1854-4
Kindle ISBN: 978-1-5051-1855-1
ePUB ISBN: 978-1-5051-1856-8

Published in the United States by
TAN Books
PO Box 269
Gastonia, NC 28053
www.TANBooks.com

Printed in the United States of America

Mike Aquilina, EWTN host and author of over 70 published books

Why would a good and all-powerful God allow us to endure suffering and evil? There is no greater challenge to faith—no unbeliever's question more urgent—and perhaps no contemporary response more persuasive than Steve Hemler's. This is essential reading for modern apologists. It is rewarding reading for anyone who has suffered or shared another person's suffering.

Karlo Broussard, Catholic Answers Staff Apologist and Speaker, author of *Purgatory Is For Real: Good News About the Afterlife for Those Who Aren't Perfect Yet*

It's one thing to articulate the philosophical basis of the age-old argument from Augustine and Aquinas that God permits evil only to bring about a greater good. It's another to complement such philosophical evidence with empirical evidence that God does in fact do that in the lives of ordinary people like you and me. In this book, Steve Hemler does just that and provides the one-two punch of philosophy and testimonials in addressing the problem of evil.

Matt Nelson, Assistant Director of the Word on Fire Institute and author of *Just Whatever: How to Help the Spiritually Indifferent Find Beliefs that Really Matter*

Though it is one of the oldest objections against the existence of a loving God, the problem of evil still remains among the most formidable obstacles to Christian faith. Intertwining personal narrative with logical argument,

Steve Hemler artfully demonstrates how we can make sense of God in a world that knows the existence of pain and evil all too well.

Rose Sweet, Catholic author, speaker, and Life Coach

Who doesn't love a compelling, inspiring story, especially one with a divine twist at the end? Steve does a masterful job of revealing the gifts that rise up from some of the most evil, painful, and personal sufferings of people just like you and me. I will definitely recommend this book to all my coaching clients who struggle with the brokenness of their lives and the question, "Why."

Rev. Michael Foley is Pastor of Our Lady of the Woods Parish in Orland Park, Illinois, and author of Walk Humbly With Your God

Steve Hemler presents a well articulated exploration of the mystery of suffering in our lives. This book explores both events within nature and through human intervention which cause suffering in this world. He does so with sound Catholic theology and real life human experiences. This thoughtful book can assist those who are wrestling with the question of human suffering both within their lives and those they love, as well as those who simply want a more thoughtful explanation of this topic.

CONTENTS

ACKNOWLEDGEMENTS

I gratefully acknowledge the many contributions of family and friends in the development of this book. I am very appreciative of Sr. Mary Margaret Ann Schlather and Catholic Distance University for implementing a new apologetics seminar on suffering, as it was this three-week-long, online seminar that prompted me to adapt my apologetics presentation on this topic into the text-based lecture format that is the basis of much of this book. I am also most grateful to several participants in that first seminar on suffering who shared their heartfelt and inspiring stories in this book—namely, Martha Madri, Bob Kaput, Richard McLeon, and Terri Thomas. I also appreciate my overseas friends Marjoe Siongco and Aneel Aranha sharing their testimonies. I am most grateful for the love and support of my wife, Linda, son Jonathan and his wife, Kelly, son Christopher and his wife, Kaila, and daughter Allison. I have been truly blessed with a terrific family. May God bless everyone involved in this labor of love and all who read this book.

This book is dedicated to the memory of John Moorehouse, editor of TAN Books, who unexpectedly passed away in December 2020 at age fifty-one. John was a true pleasure to work with and an inspiration to all who encountered him. May John rest in the peace of Christ and may his family find strength and comfort in their Catholic Faith.

INTRODUCTION

This book provides a Catholic response to the big question, "Why would a loving God allow evil, pain, and suffering?" We all wonder why bad things happen to good people, and many wonder why bad things happen at all. Watching a relative slowly die of cancer, losing a child during pregnancy, seeing addiction wreck a friend's life—suffering like this can cause us to wonder why God doesn't step in and stop these problems.

Since he's God, it seems God could stop the suffering many people experience—from physical pain (such as from disease or illness), mental anguish (such as from the death of a loved one), and natural disasters (such as hurricanes, earthquakes, fires, floods, tornadoes), as well as from evil human behavior (e.g., crime, injustice, war). Since God is loving and compassionate, then why is there so much undeserved suffering in this world? And since God is all-powerful, why doesn't God intervene and stop bad things from happening in the world and to us?

Why God allows undeserved suffering is a mystery. No explanation seems to fully satisfy our human desire for understanding. This conundrum, traditionally called

1

the "problem of evil," is an ancient difficulty, one that people have struggled with for millennia.

This book, therefore, looks at how the greatest Christian thinkers of all time have dealt with the problem of pain and the mystery of suffering. We will explore possible reasons why God might allow suffering that have been proposed by theologians throughout Church history, including how suffering can help us grow in character by finding a deeper perspective and more meaningful purpose in life.

God does not want us to suffer and does not directly cause our suffering. He is not distant and uncaring. Rather, God holds us in the highest empathy and compassion during our suffering. Nevertheless, God allows us to suffer like any parent allows their child to go to school and into the real world—to make their own decisions, including mistakes. God also permits suffering so we can learn to be courageous in the face of fear, restrained in the face of desire, compassionate with those who are hurting, and choose to love God more than the things of this world.[1]

A dominant message in our increasingly secular culture is that suffering is irredeemable, worthless, and to be avoided at all costs. However, the type of lifestyle that is focused on worldly success and having a good time will crumble in the face of life's inevitable pain and suffering. But this is no reason to despair or become bitter.

Christians today and saints throughout history have shown how God brings good out of suffering and how suffering provides an opportunity for personal and spiritual growth. We can better endure the ordeals that come our way if we, like them, develop the practice of suffering with Jesus and focus on how deeply he cares about us and our own suffering today. As such, this book will help us understand what it means to suffer well. It seems there is nothing more foreign to the modern mind than this.

The problem of evil is not merely a theoretical problem but an intensely personal one because everyone experiences pain and suffering in life. Therefore, this book includes the inspiring personal testimonies of several Catholics who have dealt positively with significant suffering in their own lives. We will see how suffering can teach us spiritual truths, build our character, and draw us closer to God, others, and the Church. Understanding the purpose of suffering can help us and those we love become better, rather than bitter, when facing life's hardships and difficulties.

Part I

SUFFERING FROM DISEASE AND NATURAL DISASTERS

Chapter 1

WHY DOES GOD ALLOW NATURAL EVIL?

Let's first look at the "big question" of why a loving God would allow disease and natural disasters, which is sometimes termed natural evil or physical evil. Typical examples of natural evil are natural disasters (such as hurricanes, tornados, floods, and earthquakes), illnesses (such as cancer and Alzheimer's), and disabilities (such as blindness and deafness). Why God allows natural evil, for which human beings cannot reasonably be blamed, is a mystery. But let's look at some possible reasons.

Suffering as a Wake-Up Call

One reason God allows us to experience pain, disease, tragedy, disappointment, and failure in life is because God is able to bring about a greater good from them. It may sound odd, but difficulties and hardships can be blessings in disguise. That's because they can be a catalyst for achieving new heights in our personal and spiritual lives. But how can this be?

We may not like to admit it, but most people are naturally self-centered. Most of us want to be self-sufficient and in control of our lives. We do not want anyone telling us what to do, and this may include God. However, in times of difficulty and hardship, we may turn to God and seek his help.

That's because for many people, God is not a "fair weather friend" but a "bad weather friend" to be called upon mainly during the hard times in life. God is often viewed as some kind of vague emergency service who is needed only when the going gets tough or when we have some kind of need. Therefore, if everything was always wonderful, do you think we would seek God or need him? Probably not, since many of us will not turn to God as long as there is any other place to look for happiness.

Our pride and desire to be in control of our life mean that we typically will not surrender our self-will to God as long as we believe all is well. Our Creator, however, has an eternal perspective that we lack and knows that our true happiness and ultimate well-being are found in being united in love with him in heaven for all eternity. Only after we surrender our will to God can we find true joy and happiness in this life, as well as the next. Yet we will typically not give our life to God as long as it remains pleasant.

C. S. Lewis addressed this in his book *The Problem of Pain*:

> Everyone has noticed how hard it is to turn our thoughts to God when everything is going well with

us. . . . Now God, who has made us, knows what we are and that our happiness lies in Him. Yet we will not seek it in Him as long as He leaves us any other resort where it can even plausibly be looked for. While what we call "our own life" remains agreeable we will not surrender it to Him. What then can God do in our interests but make "our own life" less agreeable to us, and take away the plausible source of false happiness?[2]

John Stonestreet, when reflecting on how we often go to great lengths to keep God and thoughts of death at bay, had this to say:

Years ago, when my grandfather was dying, he suffered terribly for about three or four months. In sorrow, I remember asking my pastor, "Why doesn't God just take him?"

Honestly, I expected my pastor to say something along the lines of, "Well, God has His ways, and His own timing." But he said something more important that I'll never forget: "Because your grandfather," he said, "needs to know his mortality before he meets his maker."[3]

Our illusion of self-sufficiency and self-control must, for our own sake, be shattered. Pain and suffering often shatter this illusion. For our own good, we may need to be reminded that we are not really in control of our own lives. The dark times of suffering and upheaval can shake us and cause us to reexamine who we are and what we are doing with our lives. Suffering can help us focus on the truly important things and let go of the unnecessary "clutter" in our lives.

Suffering can be a big wake-up call and bring us humbly before God. For we naturally seek God when we are walking through the valleys in our life. As C. S. Lewis also noted, *"God whispers to us in our pleasures, speaks in our conscience, but shouts in our pain: it is His megaphone to rouse a deaf world"* (emphasis added).[4]

When we suffer, we start looking deeper into ourselves, and it is in the lowest moments that we reach out to God to help us get through troubled times. Pain and suffering are a reminder of our dependency upon an all-loving Creator who wants us to be in full union with him. What other choice does God have when we continue to seek our own desires and look for happiness in all the wrong places?

As stated in the *Catechism of the Catholic Church*, "Illness and suffering have always been among the gravest problems confronted in human life. In illness, man experiences his powerlessness, his limitations, and his finitude. Every illness can make us glimpse death. Illness can lead to anguish, self-absorption, sometimes even despair and revolt against God. It can also make a person more mature, helping him discern in his life what is not essential so that he can turn toward that which is. Very often illness provokes a search for God and a return to him" (1500–1).

It is important to recognize that God does not directly cause our suffering or make us suffer just so we will love him. True love cannot be forced in that way. Rather, God allows us to suffer so that we will recognize our dependence upon him and choose to grow closer to him. We all need to realize that we are absolutely dependent upon God whether things are going well or going poorly. However, for those who do not yet have that realization, suffering can become a path to an awareness of who is really in control.

Pope Francis made this point while praying for an end to the coronavirus pandemic during the extraordinary urbi et orbi (to the city and the world) blessing on March 27, 2020 in the empty, rainy, and dark St. Peter's square:

> The [coronavirus] storm exposes our vulnerability and uncovers those false and superfluous certainties around which we have constructed our daily schedules, our projects, our habits and priorities. It shows us how we have allowed to become dull and feeble the very things that nourish, sustain and strengthen our lives and our communities. The tempest lays bare all our prepackaged ideas and forgetfulness of what nourishes our souls; all those attempts that anesthetize us with ways of thinking and acting that supposedly "save" us, but instead prove incapable of putting us in touch with our roots. . . . You [God] are calling on us to seize this time of trial as a time of choosing. It is not the time of your judgment, but of our judgment: a time to choose what matters and what passes away, a time to separate what is necessary from what is not. It is a time to get our lives back on track with regard to you, Lord, and to others.[5]

Randall's Story

Physical or emotional pain and suffering can be the means by which we become motivated to give ourselves to God and to seek what God desires to happen in our lives. This is exemplified by former atheist Randall in his powerful conversion story:

> I was a practicing atheist for nearly twenty years of my life. As a lawyer and businessman I focused everything on materialism and secular success. I had no time for emotional things, spiritual things, and I liked it that way. There was nothing that was going to get in the way of that. Unknown to me, during those twenty years my precious mom constantly prayed for me. She was praying that anything would reach me, anything would reveal God to me.
>
> It was in late 1999, actually, that my mom found herself in a battle with cancer. At that time, I was helping her out and attending oncology appointments with her. There was one oncology appointment, where in one instant, I actually had my atheism just shattered. It was just one instant of pain and just seeing her pain that the reality of life and the truth of God was just there before me. I didn't know who this God was. And, I didn't know how to reach Him. But I knew He was there at that point in time. I started praying. I didn't know who I was praying to. But I started praying for mom and her painful trial. And, at that time my heart started

opening up to also look at the claims of Jesus Christ and the claims of the Bible. I was absolutely stunned by the evidence.

On Mother's Day 2000, I gave my life to Jesus and it was that day that my mom's twenty years of patient prayer were answered. It was also that day where her battle with cancer, her painful trial, was given meaning. I think when you look at why does a loving God allow bad things to happen to good people, I think my mom actually summed it up best in one of her last journal entries before she died.

She said, "God does answer prayers in mysterious ways and does answer a mother's most fervent prayers for the soul of her beloved son. What a grand purpose for my cancer. I agree with Paul in Romans 8, for I consider that the sufferings of this present age are not worthy to be compared with the glory that shall be revealed in us."

I know in my heart that, like Christ, my mom suffered and died for me. As hard as that was for me to understand and comprehend, I now view it through more eternal goggles. I now see meaning and purpose and hope in my life, and I made the best decision I ever could have.[6]

As this personal testimony illustrates, we are not just imperfect people who need to be improved, but "rebels who must lay down our arms."[7] What else can God do but allow our lives to become more difficult and take away false sources of happiness?

Until we feel that empty ache, the helpless yearning, such as someone who is addicted to drink or drug experiences, we are stuck and cannot save ourselves. It is often when we hit bottom and finally surrender to God that we can make real progress in rising above our trials and troubles. That's because the times that bring us to our knees can bring us closer to God.

Suffering reminds us how much we need God. God often allows pain and suffering to help us find the proper perspective in life—that we are not fully in control of our lives and God is all we need. *We may not realize that God is all we need until God is all we've got.*[8]

Suffering Can Bring Us Closer to God

Suffering helps us realize that we need to give God more of our attention and our love. When we suffer, we often begin our conversations with God by asking, "Why is this happening to me?" Maybe in some way this is how God is asking us to pray more and connect with him in a deeper way.

God, in his sovereign mercy, sometimes uses our physical pain and emotional hurts to awaken in us our desperate spiritual need for him. This was addressed by Bill McGarvey in the Jesuit magazine *America*, "It is through suffering that we are broken down and made to confront our own weakness and vulnerability. This can be a transformative moment, in which we recognize at some deeper level that we are not the center of the universe. It is a moment that either opens us up to a journey in which we move beyond ourselves to see a profound connection between our suffering and the suffering of others, or it marks the beginning of a desperate attempt to reclaim our centrality in the universe."[9]

Indeed, suffering has been the cause of the conversion of many saints throughout history. Pope St. John Paul addressed this in his apostolic letter *On the Christian Meaning of Human Suffering*, "Down through the centuries and generations it has been seen that in suffering there is concealed a particular power that draws a person interiorly close to Christ, a special grace. To this grace many saints, such as Saint Francis of Assisi, Saint Ignatius of Loyola and others, owe their profound conversion. A result of such a conversion is not only that the individual discovers the salvific meaning of suffering but above all that he becomes a completely new person."[10]

It took being locked up as a prisoner of war in a grim dungeon for over a year for Francis of Assisi to find joy in God.[11] After being freed, he voluntarily gave up his previous life of wealth and luxury and embraced life as a poor itinerant preacher. Others joined him and they eventually founded several new religious communities, which have drawn countless people closer to Christ for more than eight hundred years.

And it was while being bedridden for several months after being struck by a cannonball in the leg that Ignatius of Loyola experienced his profound conversion.[12] He had dreamed of glory on the battlefield, but instead, he heard God's call and started down a new path in life. This included founding a new religious order, the Society of

Jesus (Jesuits), which has also drawn countless people closer to Christ for nearly five hundred years.

As the lives of these famous saints and many other people attest, God is wise enough to know that we need some pain and suffering, for reasons we may not fully understand, but which God knows is necessary for our eventual good. In other words, God allows short-term suffering for our long-term good. To quote the modern adage, "No pain, no gain."

Jesus himself even told us, "If any man would come after me, let him deny himself and take up his cross daily and follow me" (Lk 9:23). Jesus said we cannot be his follower unless we take up our cross with him every day. If we want to be with Jesus, we are to be with him in suffering.

Suffering and pain are not necessarily the same as harm because they can make us stronger in ways that we did not understand beforehand. It is just like a young child being given a vaccination shot. All the child knows is that it hurts. She does not understand that this temporary pain is ultimately for her own good. In the same way, God may allow suffering and hardship in order to help us move towards a greater good—spiritual maturity and eternal life in heaven.

It is understandably difficult to always have this perspective when going through tough times. For some people, faith is strengthened in adversity, while for others, hope and faith seem to be dashed. But allowing feelings of despair or anger towards God to overwhelm us is not healthy. Instead of becoming bitter or merely seeking a human solution, we do well when we turn to God for help and strength in times of trial and trouble. Sometimes, it is the pain that enables God's grace to feel so good. Difficulty is often the path that brings inner joy and wholeness.

Joni's Story

This is vividly illustrated by the testimony of Joni Eareckson Tada, who was paralyzed from the shoulders down in a diving accident when she was seventeen years old.[13] During two years of rehabilitation, she struggled with anger, depression, suicidal thoughts, and had serious religious doubts. But through her physical, emotional, and spiritual struggles, Joni eventually learned to trust in God, and this led to a very active ministry. She has written dozens of books, recorded several musical albums, starred in an autobiographical movie of her life (*Joni*), and is an advocate for disabled people. She shares her testimony:

> When I was first injured, I imagined myself as a human guinea pig lying there on my Stryker frame. I was doing nothing but eating and breathing and sleeping, and really just existing. And, I thought, "Most people out beyond these hospital walls are going to college, getting married, having children, going to work, and I'm just lying here sleeping, breathing, eating. And I realized, oh my goodness, upon my life all the truths of the human race are going to be tested. Is there a God? Does He care? What's the purpose in life? And, if there is no God,

then why not have my girlfriend slit my wrists? Why not take my mother's sleeping pills? Why not end it all? I mean who can face a life of total paralysis?"

And somewhere in there, in my anger and frustration, I realized life's got to be more than just getting born, and growing old and then dying. There has got to be a God who cares. We are too significant. There must be meaning in all of this. I don't think I would have asked those larger than life questions were it not for my suffering.

There are a lot of people who think I am a strong person. And, I'm not. I am such a weak person. I wake up in the morning and, honestly, I think, "Oh Lord, I don't have the strength for this. I am so tired. I am so tired of this paralysis." But when I start to feel overwhelmed, I'll say, "Oh God, I have no strength for this day. But, You do. I have no resources, but You do. May I please have Your resources. May I please have Your strength. I can do all things through You if You strengthen me. Please let me borrow Your smile for the day."

And, honestly, before the morning has hardly begun, I've already got a perspective on the day. I have already got peace in my heart and a mission to accomplish. And, it's because I have been pushed up against God. And, God has shown me some deep things about His purpose and Himself that, for me, are so satisfying, so pleasurable that I wouldn't trade the wheelchair for anything.[14]

Isn't it astounding that Joni actually says she "wouldn't trade the wheelchair for anything"? Of course, it has not been easy for Joni. As she shares, "Every single morning when I wake up I need Jesus so badly. I just can't tolerate the thought of another day as a quadriplegic with someone else giving me a bed bath and exercising my legs and toileting routines. It all just seems too overwhelming." And yet Joni perseveres, continually crying out to God for support.

The suffering she experiences brings humility and a new perspective. Because of her paralysis, she discovered the presence and love of God in a way that most of us have not. Joni is quite certain it is because of her suffering that she has grown as a person and found true happiness and joy by coming closer to God. As she shares, "It sounds incredible, but I really would rather be in this wheelchair knowing Jesus as I do than be on my feet without Him."[15]

Joni's personal testimony shows how God can enable good to emerge from suffering—if we run towards God, instead of away from him. When calamities or trials threaten to overwhelm us, how will we respond? Our challenge is to respond with trust and hope in God's love, care, and presence with us. The power of faith can bring confidence that we are being guided and cared for, even when that guidance and care are not immediately apparent. Faith can provide the courage and patience we need to face trauma, sickness, and even death with hope and without despair.

We know from experience that no one can escape the inevitable trials of life—pain, suffering, sickness, and death. When we encounter hardships, grief, or tragic loss, our challenge is how we will respond. With fear or with faith? With passive resignation or with patient hope and trust in God?

Jesus asks us to trust him in all things. He said, "Let not your hearts be troubled; believe in God, believe also in me" (Jn 14:1). And as Jeremiah the prophet stated, "Blessed is the man who trusts in the LORD, whose trust is the LORD" (Jer 17:7). But what does it mean to trust, to have hope, to turn our hearts to God? It means to focus the whole of our life in God and not to focus on the things of this world, such as money, power, pleasure, possessions, and prestige. Suffering has the power to bring about a new perspective on what is truly important in our lives.

It also helps to remember, as Joni does, that God never gives us more than we can handle, with his help. We will never have to suffer more than we can endure if we have faith and trust in God. As St. Paul promised, "God is faithful, and he will not let you be tempted beyond your strength, but with the temptation will also provide the way of escape, that you may be able to endure it" (1 Cor 10:13). When we are rooted in God, we can bear any burden because we are linked to and strengthened by that great power and person who created the entire cosmos.

The entire point of religion is to make us humble before God and to open us to the path of love. Suffering has the power to do that. It is through suffering that we can learn to rely on God and to trust in God's plans for us in a deeper way. It helps to remember that every trial can be a blessing in disguise and bring us closer to God—if we let it. Our pain does not have to pull us away from God, it can pull us closer.

The Witness of Those Who Suffer

When a person who is suffering maintains hope in God and belief that there will be no more suffering when this life is over but only happiness for those who die in friendship with God, this person's suffering becomes a powerful witness of faith and may lead to the conversion of others. When someone sees us maintaining our peace, even when the seas of life are getting choppy all around us, this can lead them to ask the reason for our hope (see 1 Pt 3:15). We can then point them to the grace of Jesus Christ and the love of God that is active in our lives, even in the midst of our suffering.

St. Rose of Lima, the sixteenth-century South American hermit who is patroness of the Americas, wrote of the knowledge she received about the unfathomable treasure of divine grace that comes to us through affliction, tribulation, and struggle:

> Our Lord and Savior lifted up his voice and said with incomparable majesty: "Let all men know that grace comes after tribulation. Let them know that without the burden of afflictions it is impossible to reach the height of grace. Let them know that the gifts of grace increase as the struggles increase. Let men take care not to stray and be deceived. This is the only true stairway to paradise, and without the cross they can find no road to climb to heaven."

When I heard these words, a strong force came upon me and seemed to place me in the middle of a street, so that I might say in a loud voice to people of every age, sex and status: "Hear, O people; hear, O nations. I am warning you about the commandment of Christ by using words that came from his own lips: We cannot obtain grace unless we suffer afflictions. We must heap trouble upon trouble to attain a deep participation in the divine nature, the glory of the sons of God and perfect happiness of soul."

"If only mortals would learn how great it is to possess divine grace, how beautiful, how noble, how precious. How many riches it hides within itself, how many joys and delights! No one would complain about his cross or about troubles that may happen to him, if he would come to know the scales on which they are weighed when they are distributed to men."[16]

Thomas à Kempis wrote a book over five hundred years ago entitled *The Imitation of Christ*. This book, which has become a Christian classic, describes the spiritual value of suffering and hardship. In it, he wrote:

When you are troubled and afflicted, then is the time to gain merit. You must pass through fire and water before you come to refreshment. . . . Submit yourself to the will of God, and bear whatever shall happen to you for the glory of Jesus Christ, because after winter comes summer; after the night the day returns; after the storm comes a great calm. . . . In

the cross (suffering) there is the completion of virtue; in the cross there is the perfection of sanctity.
There is no health for the soul nor hope of eternal
life, except in the cross. Therefore, take up your
cross and follow Jesus and you will attain eternal
life. . . . If you are his companions in suffering, you
shall also be partakers in his glory.[17]

Throughout the past two thousand years, many
saints and Christians, including St. Francis of Assisi and
St. Ignatius of Loyola, have shown how their suffering
brought them closer to God and enabled them to grow
in holiness. Some other such saints include St. Anthony
of Egypt, St. John of the Cross, St. Bernadette of Lourdes,
St. Thérèse of Lisieux, and St. Teresa of Calcutta. If we try
to follow their examples, we can trust this will be true in
our case too.

They have shown how God uses suffering to help us
become more virtuous and loving and enable us to help
others be more virtuous and loving, as well as how God
allows suffering to bring us and others into an eternal
life of his unconditional love and joy. When we recognize this, we can transform our suffering from an isolat-
ing and embittering experience into an opportunity for
growth and self-gift.[18]

God Brings Good Out of Suffering

St. Augustine summarized the mystery of suffering well
when he stated, "For God judged it better to bring good
out of evil than not to permit any evil to exist."[19] Even

though God does not directly cause suffering, God can bring good out of it in many ways, including developing our personal character and virtues.

Natural disasters, disease, and illness present us with the opportunity to help others and thereby develop within ourselves the virtues of compassion, unselfishness, charity, generosity, etc. Our own suffering allows us to develop the virtues of courage, patience, humility, endurance, etc. Developing these virtues would be more difficult, if not impossible, in a perfect world totally free of pain and suffering.

Our own suffering can help us develop a deeper understanding of people and their pain. This helps us be more compassionate and sympathetic to others, with a greater capacity to love. God made us for community, and having deep empathy and the opportunity to help those in need builds bonds of love. When someone is grieving or in shock, they often do not want to hear words of encouragement. Just being with them and patiently holding their pain with them is sometimes all we can do to help.

As Christians, we are called to help those who are suffering, even if they brought it on themselves through their own fault or negligence. Our love and concern in helping those who are suffering needs to be real and practical. Good intentions, showing pity, or merely empathizing with others are not enough (see Jas 2:14–17).

Our compassionate love for others must be as wide and as inclusive as is God's love. God excludes no one from his care and concern. God's love is unconditional.

So, too, we must be ready and willing to do good for others who are suffering, just as God is good to us.

Offering Up Our Suffering

When facing our own suffering, we can also "offer it up" for the good of others.[20] This means that our suffering can be united with the suffering of Christ on the cross for the salvation of the world. As stated in the *Youth Catechism of the Catholic Church*, "Christians should not seek suffering, but when they are confronted with unavoidable suffering, it can become meaningful for them if they unite their suffering with the sufferings of Christ."[21] St. Peter also advised, "Beloved, do not be surprised at the fiery ordeal which comes upon you to prove you, as though something strange were happening to you. But rejoice in so far as you share Christ's sufferings, that you may also rejoice and be glad when his glory is revealed" (1 Pt 4:12–13).

If we offer up our suffering to God, uniting it to Christ's sacrificial offering, then we are cooperating with God's divine providence and God's divine plan to bring about a greater good. Fr. Paul Scalia reflects on this:

> Everyone suffers. But not everyone sacrifices. Suffering is the simple experience of physical illness, injury, disease, and so on. We all encounter that. Sacrifice, on the other hand, is the offering of this suffering in union with Christ. Saint Paul was the first to articulate this theology of suffering: "Now I rejoice in my sufferings for your sake, and in my

flesh I am filling up what is lacking in the afflictions of Christ on behalf of his body, which is the church" (Colossians 1:24).

What has come to be called "redemptive suffering" begins with the awareness that Christ suffered first and most of all, that all our suffering must be seen in light of His. Then we recall that He is present to us in our suffering such that He shares our suffering and we share His. He is not a mere observer but has drawn close, taken our suffering upon Himself, and remains with us in the midst of it. Finally, our suffering becomes a sacrifice when, conscious of this union with Him, we offer it to Him.

As Saint Paul told the Colossians that he offered his sufferings "for your sake," so also we should offer ours for specific intentions. As He hung upon the Cross, enduring the extreme of suffering, our Lord saw each and every one of us . . . every struggle . . . every wound . . . every hurt . . . every need . . . and He offered His sufferings for us. Attaching to our offering a particular person, group, or situation helps to give meaning to our suffering and to unite it more perfectly to His. When we do so our suffering ceases to be merely that and becomes through, with, and in Christ an offering to the Father.[22]

When we take up our cross with Jesus, our suffering is transformed into a means for our sanctification and the salvation of the world. This understanding (called "the redemptive nature of suffering") has been an integral part of Christian discipleship for centuries. As Pope St. John Paul II wrote in his apostolic letter on suffering:

> The witnesses of the New Covenant speak of the greatness of the Redemption, accomplished through the suffering of Christ. The Redeemer suffered in place of man and for man. Every man has his own share in the Redemption. Each one is also called to share in that suffering through which the Redemption was accomplished. He is called to share in that suffering through which all human suffering has also been redeemed. In bringing about the Redemption through suffering, Christ has also raised human suffering to the level of the Redemption. Thus each man, in his suffering, can also become a sharer in the redemptive suffering of Christ.[23]

Of course, absolutely nothing was lacking in Christ's suffering, and his sacrificial death on the cross is sufficient for the salvation of the whole world. God does not need us to add our sufferings to those of his Son. Rather, God allows us to do so in order that we may participate more fully in Christ's suffering and unite our own suffering with his. It's like a child assisting a parent at some task that the parent is fully capable of accomplishing on their own, but the parent allows the child to participate so the child can be part of the final product.

Monsignor Charles Pope has this to say:

> Although we live forward in time from Christ's passion, we were still mystically, but really and truly, present on that day. It is in this sense that we

are "filling up what is lacking in the afflictions of Christ." It is only lacking in the sense that our share of the Passion is extended in time. When our time comes, we fulfill our role and endure our share of the Passion. This fills the gap in the Passion that waited for us, even as other gaps will be filled by those who come after us to fill up their portion. So there is nothing lacking in the perfect sacrifice of Jesus as such (cf. Hebrews 10:10-14). It is just that the portions assigned to all the future members of the full Body of Christ are yet to be realized. It is our part that is "lacking," not Jesus' part.[24]

As members of Christ's Mystical Body (the Church), we are able to unite our sufferings and sacrifices to Christ's so they take on an infinite value for the redemption of the world. Author Julie Onderko reflects on this: "Often those who are aging and suffering do not unite their pain with the redemptive work Jesus did on the cross. Bishop Fulton Sheen lamented the 'wasted suffering' when he would pass by a hospital. He knew that some of the most important work for the salvation of souls could be done from a hospital bed. We are invited to share in the redemptive work of Christ with our own suffering—what an amazing privilege!"[25]

We can offer up our suffering as a sacrifice of love to God when we endure afflictions without complaining and without despair. As St. John of the Cross stated, "Whenever anything disagreeable or displeasing happens to you, remember Christ crucified and be silent."[26]

One of the best ways Catholics can "offer up" our suffering is to offer it to God as a sacrifice during Mass. For example, during the preparation of the gifts when the priest prays, "Pray, brothers and sisters, that *my sacrifice and yours* may be acceptable to God, the almighty Father," we can consciously offer up our suffering as a sacrifice to God.

Natural Disasters and God's Providential Plan

Furthermore, the human misery and suffering that results from natural disasters is sometimes linked to immoral human behavior (moral evil).[27] For example, the results of earthquakes and hurricanes are often more disastrous in poor and underdeveloped countries with substandard buildings, such as Haiti, than in more prosperous nations. This poverty is frequently exacerbated by the exploitation of an elitist upper class that has left the masses living in substandard housing. Therefore, the results of natural disasters are often made much worse because of evil human behavior.

It is also important to recognize that natural disasters, such as earthquakes, fires, tornadoes, hurricanes, etc., are not a direct judgment or punishment of God.[28] Rather, natural disasters can be a normal by-product of a universe operating according to certain natural laws, like plate tectonics or weather systems. The same characteristics in our atmosphere that give us rain can also give us hurricanes. Our environment had to be constructed in such a way as to promote the flourishing of life, and it just so happens that the best combination of atmospheric factors to accomplish this can also produce hurricanes on occasion.

Earthquakes are due to plate tectonics, which is also essential to the flourishing of life on our planet.[29] While major earthquakes cause destruction and suffering, this does not mean that the shift of a tectonic plate is an inherently evil event. Rather, it is the by-product of a world operating according to natural laws that make life on earth possible.

God permits these things to occur because they fit into God's providential plan for human history. As discussed earlier, if we lived in a world totally free of pain and suffering, we would likely be spoiled, pampered brats who would ignore God and have no need of God whatsoever.[30]

While it is unfortunate, the reality is that people are more likely to come to know, love, and serve God, the source of true joy and eternal happiness, in a world that experiences natural disasters and disease. The fact that we live in a world with natural disasters and disease is not inconsistent with God's love and sovereignty.

God is Lord of his creation and is indeed present to us in our suffering. *God's purpose for allowing suffering is always to draw some good out of it.* We can trust that God is accomplishing a "good work" in us, though the nature and exact trajectory of that work may remain obscure to us.[31] As Joni Eareckson Tada adds, "*God permits what He hates to accomplish what He loves.*"[32]

It is not that God wants us to suffer, but God knows that suffering provides us with the opportunity to cooperate with God's grace in our lives and experience deep blessings. Suffering forces the decision as to whether we will sink into bitterness and despair or seek to trust in God and grow in virtue. If we let him, God will use our suffering to draw us closer to him and develop our character.

How some people have experienced this in their own suffering is what we will explore in subsequent chapters. The suffering and loss we read about in these true, personal stories may seem so senseless and unnecessary. But we will also read in these inspiring stories about the good that God can bring about from suffering and loss. We will hear real stories of how God provides strength to persevere in the toughest of times, companionship to remind us that we are never alone, hope that we will meet our deceased loved ones again, and true love as we walk the journey of faith in this life.

Chapter 2

MY STRENGTH AND MY REST

This chapter is the story of Marjoe and Jean Siongco's journey in faith that they experienced during the time they worked and lived in Saudi Arabia, including Jean's battle with cancer.

My name is Marjoe (Mario Jose) Siongco and I am from the Philippines. I come from a family of five children that were raised as Roman Catholics and went to schools mainly run by the Augustinian Recoletos and the Dominican friars. At the University of Santo Tomas, where I went for my college degree, I met my wife, Jean (Virginia) Lim. We were both enrolled at the College of Commerce, majoring in accounting. I met Jean through a classmate who happened to be her dorm mate. From there on, I was love struck and pursued to court her.

Jean comes from a Chinese family from Vigan, Ilocos Sur, a city four hundred kilometers north of Manila. She is the second child in the family, like me. During our university days, it was sort of a long distance relationship every time school was closed. However, this did not discourage me to continue pursuing the relationship, and she turned out to be my college sweetheart on April 5, 1973 leading up to our graduation in 1976. We both took and passed the Certified Public Accountant (CPA) board exam the following year and got employed thereafter.

Our Early Life in Saudi Arabia

In 1979, I left Manila for Saudi Arabia to work for the Arabian American Oil Company (now Saudi Aramco). This was a decision made by us as a prelude to our plan of saving and settling down. After a year, I returned home and married Jean on December 1, 1980. She followed me to Saudi Arabia a year after and found herself also working at the same company.

How happy we were and fortunate that aside from having work, we were also able to practice our Christian faith. Though there are no physical church buildings in Saudi Arabia, a Catholic parish does exist—Our Lady of the Rosary of Fatima. This religious privilege is due to a verbal royal decree granted by the first Saudi king to the company.

Through the years as we progressed with our lives in Saudi Arabia, we were blessed with our first child, Mark Angelo, who was born on April 5, 1983. It's funny how God blessed us to have Mark born exactly on the same date (April 5) that Jean had become my fiancée. Three years later, we were likewise blessed to have a daughter, Angela Kay, who was born on November 6, 1986.

Both Mark and Kay got baptized, confirmed, and received the sacraments of Penance (confession) and Holy Eucharist (Communion) while in Saudi Arabia. Their knowledge of God was nurtured through the religious education classes provided by the parish. As our family grew and our life in Saudi Arabia became busier, God continued to shower blessings and let us enjoy most of life's material comforts and delights.

How Our Life Changed After Jean's First Cancer

Circumstances and events later on would dramatically change course; for in 1993, Jean was diagnosed with thyroid cancer. By a mere accident, the cancer was discovered during a visit to the Aramco Clinic because of a cold and sore throat. A lump in her neck was found during the physical examination and an excision for a sample was made, which turned out to be cancerous in nature.

With our peaceful life shaken by her illness, by the word *cancer*, we turned to God for prayers of healing. A thyroidectomy operation to remove the cancerous thyroid nodules was performed. It was a tricky operation that could affect her larynx (voice box) with possibility of damaging the nerve and result in loss of voice or having a hoarse voice. Our prayers were answered, the operation was a success with no effect on her voice. As a follow up to the operation, radioactive iodine medication was prescribed.

Beforehand, we were just the average religious family out there, God fearing and weekly Mass goers. God was there to be taken at our convenience, on an as needed basis. Life then was revolving around us, what we needed, and mostly these were earthly things. One can say God was a passive part of our lives. However, this would change when we were in Saudi Arabia. God came to us when we were in pain and in suffering. How ironic that we seem to know God best when we are down and in utmost need.

When cancer hit Jean, things went in shambles, nothing that we had nor any amount of earthly possessions we owned could bring back the peace to which we were accustomed. Maybe this was God's way of stirring us, for us to know him better. We turned to him, lifted our sufferings, and prayed for healing. God came and never abandoned us. Our lives started to be normal again with our new found peace. Jean's cancer made us realize that only in prayers and communion with God do we gain peace. This paved the way to the start of our spiritual growth.

Jean was the most active and faithful one in our family, which was probably because she was the one who was physically sick. This led her to attend more prayer gatherings, and she initially joined the Legion of Mary (LOM) group with both Mark and Kay. Then came the Rosary Novena group, Our Lady of Perpetual Help, and later she became a member of a Filipino Christian Charismatic group, "Ilaw at Gabay", which in English means "Light and Guide."

I saw her transformation, her devotion to know God more and more. She was busy with religious activities, with different meetings and was full of life again. Along the way, Mark and Kay were also getting closer to Our Lord, with their participation in the Legion of Mary, etc. All of them were getting busy with their spiritual growth. I was just tagging along, an indirect participant, contributing my own humble prayers to Our Lord.

My Christian Life

Bible Scripture readings and discussions were now getting part of the daily conversations, and here I was, just listening to what my family was talking about. I knew I was growing in spirit likewise, but I was at the tail end. I recognized the kids were developing spiritually too, for nothing can take them out of the LOM meetings. If family events or social functions conflict with their LOM activities, they would rather skip these affairs and be with the LOM group. Their rooms started having more religious articles and handouts. Except for me, the family was lively in religious activities.

Six years later, in August 1999, at Jean's urging, I finally agreed to join the Christian charismatic group by attending a Life in the Spirit Seminar (LSS) on my birthday, August 27. The LSS formation talks given that day were just a start, for after that came the Praise and Worship and then the participants being prayed over. After all the talks, discussions, and Adoration activities, we were divided into two groups and formed a circle in preparation of being prayed over. And lo and behold, when it was my turn to be blessed and prayed over, I was slain in the Spirit and fell down with several hands holding unto my back to keep me from getting hurt. As I lay on the floor, my body started to shake, heart beating faster and sounds coming out of my mouth, incoherent mumbling sounds that are too foreign to me. These foreign words just keep coming out of my mouth louder and louder! It felt like I was praying to Our Lord in words that his Spirit alone can comprehend. Then I cried realizing that I just received the Gift of Tongues!

How blessed I am to receive this as a birthday present on my natal day. They say life begins somewhere in your forties, and truly for me this was a reality, for on that day my religious life took off. Going to bed that night I remember telling Jean that I was afraid to lose that feeling I just experienced. She answered back sharp as a knife—God is always there, it is us that stray away from him! From that day on I became an active member of the group, attending every prayer meeting and Bible study.

More Cancer

We did not know then that God had further plans for our spiritual journey, to again experience that dreaded, frightening word: *cancer*. Our lives were once more shaken in 2002 when Jean had her second bout with cancer; this time, tumor calcifications were detected in her right breast during a routine medical examination. She underwent lumpectomy to remove the cancerous tissues, and as in her initial thyroid cancer, we lifted again this illness to Our Lord.

We said more, many more, prayers, but this time also realizing that our faith really grows not in comfortable conditions but when we are challenged and tested. Relying on God's mercy and love, we took this cancer as a blessing. If God allowed it to happen, then there must be a purpose, a reason, and something good will come out of this sickness.

After the operation, chemotherapy with a mild drug followed as a preventive medical treatment. Over the months that went by, Jean recovered physically and continued her work at Saudi Aramco.

Our journey with Jean's illness that year brought us to the Couples for Christ (CFC) community with our charismatic group ultimately getting assimilated into this Vatican recognized organization. We became active CFC members leading our own households and giving talks at Christian Life Program seminars. At the same time, Jean likewise became busy getting herself involved in the parish council and in daily Mass activities as Liturgy Coordinator.

She also became fond of reading religious books, especially books on the lives and sufferings of the saints. And foremost over the years when her cancer was in remission, we both became Lay Eucharistic Ministers in our parish, as well as baptism and Pre-Cana (marriage) coordinators. God has provided us with the opportunity to serve back the Church and the community for all the blessings we have received.

Our hope for her full remission from cancer went up in smoke in 2006 when her breast cancer came back. Our family life was again thrown in shambles, for the CT scan and mammogram results confirmed that the cancer had now moved to her left breast. After long discussions with family members and the medical team, Jean underwent bilateral mastectomy to remove both breasts and take out all cancer tissues. This was followed by several aggressive cycles of chemotherapy that resulted in her not just losing her hair but also losing much of her body weight.

Events turned worse in early 2007 when she was diagnosed cancer stage 4 with metastases in her lungs, pelvic bones, and liver. At a time when she was recovering back her strength and gaining weight, here comes another full cycle of chemotherapy. What else can go wrong! Nothing, for as we continued with our journey, we lifted everything to Our Lord and accepted his will for us. We trusted him fully, knowing he walks with us on this journey and has the best plan laid ahead.

Deeper Growth in Faith

As our faith continued to carry us forward in spite of our brokenness and struggles, we found peace and serenity in our lives—Jean in particular. She was still full of hope and life. She never showed her pains and continued to serve both in her work and in the community. She inspired a lot of people, particularly those that were sick, including my sister Tessa who likewise was diagnosed with ovarian cancer.

Jean became active in an online cancer blog giving advice and motivating people to continue living life to the fullest even when they are suffering. How can cancer victims find happiness in their pain? Jean made me understand that it was possible through God's grace when you offer it to Christ Jesus in complement of his cross! This made me want to be sick as well, of thinking that if I was getting indirectly blessed in faith with Jean's illness, perhaps I, by being sick myself will receive a double dosage of spiritual blessings!

As she recovered and while there was still time, we decided to go on a pilgrimage trip—to know God better and to be closer to him. That same year, in late 2007, we made our first trip that brought us to Mount Nebo in Jordan and the Holy Land, with Jean barely able to keep up with the other pilgrims because of her health issues. Nevertheless, we were full of joy at being able to visit and pray in the places where Our Lord did his ministry.

As we kept on with our prayers, growing more in faith, God not only heard and answered our prayers but also led and guided us to embark into more spiritual journeys. He allowed Jean's cancer to become stable stage 4, with the metastases not moving nor increasing. She gained back her strength and was put on oral chemotherapy all the time, being on maintenance to stabilize the tumor markers.

This afforded us to make yearly pilgrimages, visiting places like Lourdes and Nevers in 2008; Assisi, Lanciano, and San Giovanni Rotondo in 2009; Fatima and Santarem in 2010; Loreto, Padova, Sienna, Cascia, and Assisi again in 2011; Orvieto and Bolsena in 2012, and Milan and Prague in 2013.

In our travels, we visited many churches and basilicas, saw incorruptible bodies of saints, and sites of

Eucharistic miracles. All of this contributed more to our spiritual development and a closer personal relationship with Our Lord. The pilgrimage trip we made in 2011 was very memorable and spiritually uplifting, as this was with Jean's siblings and their spouses.

Over those years that went by since the cancer was stable, the Oncology Clinic became our second home with the frequent tests, scans, blood transfusions, and medications that have to be taken. But all these did not prevent Jean from continuing to serve the Church and the Couples for Christ. She continued to do without fail her duties as well as her commitment to the monthly two thousand Hail Marys that she advocated in our parish every first Saturday. Jean started the Hail Mary devotion to honor our Blessed Mother, for the intercessory prayers and help she made possible during her trying pains and sufferings.

Her Increasing Suffering and Death

In April 2014, Jean's tumor markers again started to climb and the bone scan showed that the bone metastases was progressing. With this came pain in the pelvic area that kept increasing as the months passed by. It was during this time one night that the pains became so unbearable for her that she cried all night, unable to either sit or lay in bed, with standing providing the least pain. We were both just standing the whole time, embracing each other as we walked around the house for long hours calling the name of Jesus for help. The pain never left and we were both exhausted physically, so I laid over the couch with Jean resting on my chest.

We barely got sleep that night, and as soon as the Oncology Clinic opened in the morning, we asked for pain medication. She was given a drug that reduced the pain to a more bearable level. With her present pain condition, the oncologist decided to give radiation therapy to the pelvic area. Jean was given localized radiation on her pelvic bone for four consecutive days, and that completely took the pain away.

However, even without pain, her tumor markers just continued to rise just like a bull stock market on the run! To mitigate the rise, several oral chemo drugs were administered to her towards the end of 2014, but they never really worked. Finally, the oncologist decided to start an aggressive intravenous (IV) chemotherapy immediately after our return from Christmas vacation that year.

Beginning in February 2015, Jean was given chemotherapy, and after just a few cycles, the tumor markers still continued to rise. The medical team decided to discontinue the treatment and replaced it by a stronger drug, this time for a full six cycles that likewise failed to address the rising tumor markers. The same scenario with different chemo drugs continued for several months with the same results.

In December 2015, after a nonstop yearlong chemo treatment that no longer worked and took a heavy toll on her body, causing her to lose considerable weight and go frail, Jean lost her battle with cancer. She died on December 10 at God's appointed time but not before she manifested for the last time her love for prayers. The night before she died, our parish priest anointed her with the sacrament of the Anointing of the Sick while she was gasping for breath. Suddenly, in her unconsciousness, she stopped gasping for air and her lips started to move in silent prayers when we prayed for Mother Mary's intercession. They say hearing is the last to go when one is about to die, and upon hearing the Hail Mary, she was totally in union with us in prayers. The moment we ended the Hail Mary prayer, she was back again gasping for breath.

Death is something people do not want to talk about or experience, for with it comes emptiness, sadness, despair, and even anger. Not Jean. She embraced her inevitable death with happiness and zeal, for she looked forward to meeting Our Lord. All throughout her illness, our prayers were for a peaceful, painless death, and strength for the family. God, in his compassion, provided these. For Jean died feeling no pain, and in our moment of difficulty, for those she left behind, God is ever present. God allowed us to feel joy and peace when she passed away. We held onto God's promise that she who believes in him will have eternal life. God has given and he has now taken. What we lost physically, we have gained spiritually, for Jean is now among God's angels. She is in a better place and prays fervently for all of us.

In my solitude as I continue my journey, I thank God for letting me experience his love through the life of my wife. I now realize that throughout her illness, in the many events God had allowed in our lives, he and Jean were actually preparing me for that very moment of her demise—to be strong in faith and in prayer. For this is the same faith and prayerful life that she took with her when she left for heaven.

I completed forty years of work in Saudi Arabia during 2019 and retired that year. I do not know when and how my journey will end, but I fear not, for I trust that Our Lord will always be there, as before. I look back at that day in 1979 when I signed my contract of work, of seeing for the first time the letters SR—which stands for Saudi Riyals, my employment currency. Yes, I left Saudi Arabia endowed with material blessings, but much more meaningfully, I returned home blessed in spiritual richness, for it is there where I experienced the love of Christ in the very same letters of SR. I go home knowing the real treasure—Jesus Christ who is my Savior and my Redeemer; my Shield and my Refuge; my Stronghold and my Rock; and my Strength and my Rest! Praise be to God and to him be the Glory!

Chapter 3

WHAT A DEVASTATING HURRICANE

This is the testimony of Martha Madri and her struggles in dealing with the effects from Hurricane Sandy.

John and I were married in June 1975 and taught in Catholic schools throughout our marriage until our retirement in August 2020. John was a high school English teacher for forty-eight years in a prestigious Catholic high school, and I taught for forty-eight years in two different Catholic elementary schools. I taught third, fourth, and fifth grades. Both of us loved working with the children, and throughout the years, we added special lessons and afterschool classes in drama, creative writing, music, and ballet in my elementary school. For years, we put on plays that John and I wrote. One play John wrote was performed by his high school students, and the other plays we wrote were experienced by my third, fourth, or fifth grade students. I had a ballet club and a piano (keyboard) club in the past. My most recent club was the creative writing club. We taught the children to celebrate their God-given talents and enjoy sharing their skills and creativity through writing. Faith and the love of Jesus have always been part of our teaching.

Our present house is our second house, which we had bought as a mother-daughter home for my mom over twenty years ago. This house has given us problems with basement floods and groundwater ever since we have lived here. As of late, however, the basement has not flooded much, but water sometimes seeps inside both ends of the basement.

We love animals and have lived with birds, two dogs, and cats. We have done rescue work with cats and have saved many after one pregnant cat came into the basement of our other house and gave birth to five kittens. Our dog loved the cats, all six of them, so we kept them. They have all since passed on. Many feral cats have been fed by John, lived in shelters in our backyard, made touchable and friendly, and been spayed or neutered by veterinarians. Some kittens and cats have come inside our house to live, and others were adopted. People have anonymously left adult cats in front of both our present and former houses, and we took them to the vet and kept them. At one point, we had eighteen cats and kittens in our house. But many more have lived with us over the years, perhaps about fifty. I share this as background for the day that everything changed in our lives.

Before any potential natural disaster, most people pray to God to keep themselves and their beloved families and friends safe with little damage affecting their property. What if the force of a hurricane is more than expected and people are upset with their seemingly unanswered pleas for God's help to stop the devastation? Is God to be blamed? Does God listen and answer prayer? My faith says God is not the reason for destructive natural forces. God hears those who belong to him and sincerely ask for help. God doesn't abandon his people and remains with them, giving them courage to fight the storm. Hurricane Sandy greatly affected all of us in Howard Beach, New York, and surrounding communities. Unsurprisingly, this natural disaster challenged some people's faith in God's love and protection.

During the Storm

The date was October 29, 2012, the day of Hurricane Sandy, and John and I were travelling home from a day of teaching. As we approached Howard Beach, the massive thick gray clouds appeared to be darker than usual and there was a stillness in the air. Although the media warnings alerted the people in proximity of the hurricane's path of impending danger and suggested they leave their homes, John and I, our immediate neighbors, and some of those in surrounding areas didn't heed the warnings because we didn't expect what followed.

In the evening of Hurricane Sandy, three storms converged on Howard Beach and the neighboring communities, and the powerful wind created a storm surge about twelve feet high. Because our house is located a few blocks from the canal, and the saltwater overflowed into the streets, our house didn't have a chance for protection from the rising water as it travelled down the streets.

As the storm hit, there was no rain. John and I were watching a movie. There was a loud commotion of talking outside our house, horns honking, and car alarms blaring, so I went outside and stood on our front porch to see what was going on. Every head of those standing in our block was fixed to the right, looking down the street as a flow of cars was travelling in the opposite direction of the one-way street to escape the large wave of water that was rushing down the block.

I called John to come outside to see what was happening. Panic and fear filled the air as we saw the approach of a very high wave of water rushing down the block. I realized that our neighbors were attempting to save their cars by driving to safety, something we foolishly hadn't even considered. We stood mesmerized by the ghastly vision and prayed for God's protection.

The engulfing wave of water headed right down our block, passed our house, and before we realized it, made a left turn on our corner and then another sharp left turn as if purposely driven to pour down our basement steps. Like a waterfall, the water broke through two security doors, windows and locks, and inundated our basement with over seven feet of saltwater. Meanwhile, the water was rising rapidly in front of our house and heading for the front door. Thankfully, it missed our first floor by inches. As all this was happening, we invited a stray feral cat into our house, but she preferred swimming and being washed away with the waves. (We thought we had lost her, but three days later, she appeared outside for breakfast.)

During the hurricane's continuing attack that night, as we sat in the kitchen, the force of the incoming water slammed shut our inside basement door, which led to our kitchen, stopping the water from ascending the basement stairs into the main level of our home. I shuttered at the noise and prayed that our house would not be destroyed. Little did we know how God protected us with the closure of that door, because I was considering going down in the basement for a few things not realizing that the water was violently climbing with such power that furniture was being knocked about by the water. If we or the cats had been downstairs, we would have died.

As the storm progressed, the flood continued down the block to other homes. Our next-door neighbor unfortunately was switching apartments with his tenant, and he had stored all his family's belongings in his basement. As he watched the water enter his basement, he later told us he wanted to jump into the water and die. He was so upset. Most of their furniture, clothing, and his two children's toys were destroyed, but thankfully nobody was injured.

Hurricane Sandy was the most horrifying experience my husband and I have thus far lived through as we saw the tsunami-type water flowing down our block, forcibly entering our basement, breaking windows, locks, and security doors. We prayed and knew God was with us during our time of need.

As for ourselves, we had thought there would be a flood in our basement, as with most storms, but this attack was beyond our expectations and those of the people and businesses in the community. I prayed as I always did for God's protection. The storm attacked and moved on leaving us survivors, our house impaired with over seven feet of water in the basement, a destroyed car, a twisted deck, a partially flooded garage, and many suffering neighbors also facing their losses from Hurricane Sandy.

Immediately After the Storm

The morning after the storm, rescuers went through the neighborhood to bring people to shelters. I heard a knock at our front door. John and I found a bright flashlight in our eyes when firemen offered to take us to a shelter. We refused because at that time we had twelve house cats who would have died of starvation had we been taken away. We were told that the nearby shelters were full and that they didn't know where we would be taken or when we could return. That was just too risky.

Besides the cats, we had to stay in the house because all our books were there. I was completing a course in theology and needed to keep studying. Being teachers, John and I also had schoolwork to handle. We could not afford to let the perils of the hurricane disrupt our lives too much. I prayed as we suffered through all the responsibilities we had to do while trying to keep ourselves well and strong enough to do them. I also wanted to go see my mom in a nursing home, but our car was dead because of the saltwater, and we couldn't rent a car.

The following day, a police officer brought us a sleeping bag and a package of ham and cheese sandwiches. We were so grateful for food because the stores were flooded and closed. We tried to keep our limited amount of food in the refrigerator cold by not opening the door too often. We never got the chance before the storm to do our food shopping. One neighbor brought me a new robe. The neighbors looked out for each other.

Since Con Edison had turned off electricity in the area to avoid fires, the church offered people heaters, but a generator was needed to use them. However, we did not have a generator for our lights, refrigerator, or sump pumps to function. For the next five weeks, we suffered in our cold, dark house, which was lit only by flashlights. Our neighbor offered us use of a lamp connected to his generator, but we refused thinking one of our cats might bite the cord and cause more havoc. Nevertheless, we gratefully accepted his offer to charge our phones.

We had many concerns during this time with no heat or electricity. We prayed that God would protect our pipes from freezing because that October there was an early ice storm. We were thankful our pipes never froze. It was impossible to get warm even with layered clothing. We feared for our health and that of our cats.

Life was difficult for us during the following weeks. Everything in our basement was destroyed, including the furnace, hot water heater, washer, dryer, electrical wiring, furniture, books, teaching materials, clothes, children's costumes and props for plays, music books, and an original song we composed, and some soft sculpture dolls I made. When we looked at the mess from the outside doorway into our basement, we saw what looked like a war zone. The contents of the basement were a mess of disorder and filth with pieces of furniture on top of other furniture. It was so sad because some new sets of books never made it to school for the children, the music books for teaching keyboard were gone, and the costumes and props would no longer be used in our school plays.

We again realized how fleeting material things can be, since they can be taken away in one big fury of destructive power through natural forces. Whatever material possessions we have can be lost in an instant. Most precious are our lives and our faith in God's goodness and love for us, which gives meaning at the end of the day. We are to live for God and pray we follow his will. Praying at Mass and receiving the Holy Eucharist help us understand our path to God.

A few days later, we took a walk to see the damage and talk with the National Guard soldiers stationed in Howard Beach to get information about the storm and when our electricity would be restored. As we were walking, an older neighbor from around the block came out of her house complaining quite loudly that there is no God. How could there be a God who would allow the hurricane to hurt our lives? I felt sadness, as well as anger, at her accusation, so I told her that God was not to blame. People often ruin the environment by misusing nature, and this can contribute to violent weather. God loves us and doesn't desert us. He is always with us.

This was one of the most important lessons of Hurricane Sandy. Yes, God did not stop the attack, but he did give us the courage to live and accept the cross the hurricane had caused. I believe the woman was asking how a righteous and fair God would not stop the injustice of destruction given to her and her family from Hurricane Sandy. She was angry and confused. She wanted God to stop it, but he didn't. The woman didn't want to suffer. The results of the hurricane became a cross to bear. Her cry to me was a call for help and answers. I thanked God for our lives and what did remain. The unknown factors of the storm did frighten us, but we had faith that we would make it through the ordeal.

Life, however, was difficult for us during the following weeks. Most of our neighborhood suffered over a month without electricity, heat, or hot water. There were flooded basements and first floors, dead cars, and physical destruction to the homes, property, trees, and businesses. Only a few stores could open. Some people did abandon their homes and looters came. Other people who stayed warned us about men driving trucks full of supposedly boxed boilers, stoves, and refrigerators, but people who bought them found the boxes contained broken pieces of junk.

One man offered my husband a gun in case an intruder broke into our house, but he refused. We were also told that men posing as Con Edison workers got into people's homes and robbed them. Many homes near the canal were wrecked. One woman told us her boat was on top of her car because she lived adjacent to the canal. Another woman said she had fish in her basement. A professor lost his entire manuscript for a new book he was writing when his computer was destroyed by the saltwater. Another woman lost her collection of rare valuable statues she had stored in her basement. Some people cried and others were angry.

Dealing with the Aftermath

After the hurricane, our lives became a mess of massive expenses, much more than we could afford. We had to determine how we would get our basement cleaned out. People frightened us about the germs and mold. People gave us leads on help, but everyone was too busy. Our neighbor got some men with hazmat suits and a garbage truck to clean out everything we had stored in the basement and take the remains to the garbage dump. The garbage removers charged us a lot of money. All prices were higher because their services were highly in demand. Many who helped us gouged us with ridiculously high prices. But we had no choice. Our previously finished and insulated basement was destroyed and left barren.

In the following days, another person bleached our basement several times to destroy the mold. We barricaded our kitchen with tape and towels to keep the sickening smell from reaching us and our cats. Another man came around to buy scrap metal, which he then sold. He tried to convince us to remove a large piece of metal our previous owners had installed in the basement's ceiling which reinforced a section of the floor above the basement. They must have had a large fish tank to support. We refused. He then offered to paint our basement. Only the concrete walls were left, but he said the paint would prevent mold and waterproof the walls. He did some painting.

Five weeks later, the electrical box and all the wiring in the basement were changed because they were covered with salt. At this point, even our drop ceiling was removed by the electricians. After all that work, someone had to inspect the wiring to restore electricity in our house. However, we still had to wait for a new boiler and water heater. A friend got someone to pick up and install the new water heater, boiler, and washer and dryer we had bought. It was a long, tedious process.

People were good to us after Hurricane Sandy. Our friends, faculties, and priests from our two schools gave us monetary gifts, which partially paid for our new washer and dryer, boiler, and water heater. We were also given gift cards, some clothes, a couch and chair, and food. FEMA gave us money for repairs. We were fortunate to have such support, and we thanked God for the help.

Most neighborhood cars were destroyed by the salt water. We eventually leased a new Honda because we needed a car and all the rental cars were gone to other people. Those who drove experienced a gas shortage, which caused long lines of cars with people waiting for gas on odd and even distribution days. Once we were able to drive and had better access to gasoline, we went back to work, visited my mother in a nursing home, and I returned to St. John's University Graduate School to complete a course in theology.

At night, people held flashlights that looked like lightning bugs to get around. One particular night when we returned home from school, John and I saw a large lit cross on our garage door. It remained there for a few minutes even after we turned off our car lights. We couldn't find its source, but we felt that God understood our suffering. We had to persevere and bear our crosses.

The hurricane happened during a most difficult time in my life. My mom was in a nursing home. She had survived hospice twice, which was unheard of. She had recovered enough strength from God because her nurse's aide prayed for her, sang religious songs to her, and truly cared for her daily. She was a blessing. Unfortunately, the nurse's aide left that nursing home because her coworkers were unkind to her. We visited my mother as often as we could considering we needed a car and she was miles away. I continued to pray for her.

My mom always had great faith and love for Jesus Christ. However, because she was ninety-one years old and fragile, I kept much of the effects of Hurricane Sandy on our lives away from her for fear it would make her worse. Weeks after the hurricane, however, someone told her about it and she got physically worse. She went into hospice a third and final time. It was heartbreaking. The priest from my husband's school gave her last rites and prayed with her. That night, she went to her eternal home. We felt God was with her and us and helped us survive her loss.

During her ordeal, I was completing my last course in theology and preparing for the comprehensive exam to get my master's degree in theology, which I did earn. I thought I might not pass the final comprehensive test because I was so tired and couldn't remember everything clearly when I was so strained. I prayed and I felt God tell me that he would help me make it happen. He did. I had promised God that I would learn more about theology after my mom had gotten sick and could no longer live with us. I now have a master's degree in systematic theology. God does answer prayers.

The Church was always open to help those in need. God was always with us showing his love through the many people who helped us. The effects of Hurricane Sandy were not only destructive; they were insightful about the goodness of people. The suffering brought people together to work out the mess that Hurricane Sandy caused. People prayed together at Mass for those suffering from Hurricane Sandy, and because of this, we could remain strong and work together as a community to rebuild.

During the entire ordeal of Hurricane Sandy, I found support from praying, reading the Bible, and going to Mass. It was interesting how I found relevant help from Scripture. The relevancy of the Bible to our daily situations helped me to know how God speaks to us within Scripture.

One Scripture reading that helped me was the words of St. Paul in Philippians 4:12–13, "I know how to be abased, and I know how to abound; in any and all circumstances I have learned the secret of facing plenty and hunger, abundance and want. I can do all things in him who strengthens me." I needed the strength and thanked God I endured.

Another helpful Scripture reading was Philippians 4:6–7, "Have no anxiety about anything, but in everything by prayer and supplication with thanksgiving let your requests be made known to God. 7 And the peace of God, which passes all understanding, will keep your hearts and your minds in Christ Jesus." I prayed for help, protection, and guidance. As Psalm 16:1 says, "Preserve me, O God, for in you I take refuge."

And 2 Corinthians 8:9–12 spoke to me, "Though he was rich, yet for your sake he became poor, so that by his poverty you might become rich. And in this matter I give my advice: it is best for you now to complete what a year ago you began not only to do but to desire, so that your readiness in desiring it may be matched by your completing it out of what you have. For if the readiness is there, it is acceptable according to what a man has, not according to what he has not." I knew I had to resume and complete all the activities I had before Hurricane Sandy.

Some Lessons Learned

In retrospect, the times before, during, and after Hurricane Sandy can be labeled "concern" about the hurricane's immediate impact, "perseverance" during the trial of discomfort after the storm, and "reconstruction" during the rebuilding of homes and community. During the first stage of "concern," I was worried but believed we would make it through the hurricane because I had faith that God would not let us perish. Although the core of our house with the boiler, water heater, and electric system was flooded and destroyed, that destruction did not affect my faith nor wound me to the core of my being. Thank God, during the "perseverance" stage we could still function even without the comforts of warm water, heat, and electricity. The "reconstruction" stage proceeded from the kind people who gave us gifts of food, money, and clothing. My husband and I were appreciative and thankful when we were on the receiving end of their kindness and generous works of mercy.

Thinking back to the hurricane's impact on our lives, I remember not only the cold house, the lack of food, and the things destroyed. I also remember my prayerful heart thanking God for what remained and the health and strength God provided for us to withstand that ordeal. I try to remember that we should always be thankful to God, even for the next day, the air we breathe, the food we eat, the people in our lives, and for so many other reasons.

Others, not only in our immediate vicinity, have withstood cruel weather at some point and must have felt badly, as I did, about their complete dependence and personal vulnerability in not being in control of their situation. But for us, our confidence in Jesus to lift us above the chaos to a level of security was an act of pure and redeeming faith. The road could be painful, but by accepting our crosses, we find Jesus who gives us strength to endure.

This life can be full of negative influences that cause people and animals distress. Didn't Jesus come to our human situation because human beings were sick and in need of God to enlighten, forgive, and nourish them by his holy cross? Jesus offered his life to nourish the living. Jesus experienced this difficult world. God wants us saved from the death of the soul by helping us through the lives of the living.

It seems that many people learn and grow closer to God through suffering. When following their own ways of handling problems is not enough, they realize they need God and call upon him. I believe a closeness with God is always the reason for existence during good and bad times. I believe Jesus is pleased with us when decisions made in life's struggles follow his plan of righteousness, and he gives courage and peace to people who need and want him in their lives.

It is also interesting to ask if God directly allows natural disasters. It appears that God does not often intervene. We can pray for a storm to change direction or not be so severe, but does prayer always help? I believe prayer is most important even when the disaster culminates in death. In the Bible, Jesus was saddened by people's afflictions and he often made them well.

The suffering we experienced made us stronger perhaps for greater battles, but I pray they will never come to pass. God is the almighty Creator who has no need of us, yet we are brought to our knees in need of him. Through our communion with Jesus, our Savior, God allows us to help each other work through his plan of salvation for each of us with the guidance of the Holy Spirit. God created us and never abandons us. Accepting our cross and dealing with all its ramifications and demands gave me a more empathetic feeling for the suffering of others and their painful path to salvation.

After our experiences with Hurricane Sandy, I think of suffering differently. That's because I better understand how suffering can help us follow the living goodness of Jesus Christ and deal with our crosses by putting our complete trust and faith in God to improve the human condition for ourselves and others. The gift of suffering helps us better understand our human frailty and makes us humble before God. Suffering enables us to seek God's will and the path that Jesus wants us to follow in our lives.

People strive for independence and being self-sufficient in handling problems, yet suffering pierces that veneer of control and returns people to God's mercy to help them through difficult times that are beyond their control.

Suffering helps us recognize the gift of Jesus who never abandons us even through death and gives us eternal peace and happiness in heaven where only goodness, love, and mercy abide. All pain, malice, jealousy, hatred, greed, lust, and selfishness will cease when we are united in eternity with the power and light of Jesus's love for the family of humanity. With Hurricane Sandy, it was as though the entire community was forced to befriend neighbors and to help each other through their personal turmoil. Out of the storm came the strength of kindness shown through the many works of mercy.

When studying the lives of some saints, many of them willingly sacrificed food and all common comforts of everyday living to live prayerful, contemplative lives. St. Francis, St. Anthony, and St. Benedict stayed in caves to be closer to God. St. Catherine of Siena lived in a bare room in her parent's house where she prayed. These saints gave up their wills to Jesus so that they could know and follow his will. They suffered and accepted their pain. It is difficult for most people to live as they did. When we suffer on this earth, Jesus uses the pain to help us find him. Jesus is our Savior and wants salvation for all of us. He allows our suffering on Earth to bring us closer to him and give us eternal peace in heaven.

Have you ever noticed how after a dreadful storm, the next day, the sun shines its smile as if nothing unusual has happened? A storm may rage, but afterwards there is tranquility and peace. It is as if the innocence has been restored and what is gone is gone. Then we see what is truly important. Abandoning ourselves to God's mercy is most important. Suffering helps give us a new perspective on life. How much strength do we have to survive a storm? Living through a hurricane and its devastating aftermath makes a person take note of how suffering builds character and helps us relate to others with more compassion, generosity, and love.

In conclusion, hurricanes and other natural disasters can either bring people closer to God, as they realize their vulnerability and their need for God's help, or draw them away from God, as they get angry at God as though he directly caused their misery. They can either take what problems life gives them and, with God's help, become stronger or they can allow difficulties to tear them down without the strength given to them by the Holy Spirit. The choice does not belong to fate; it belongs to us. We tend to view suffering as a negative because it takes away our comfort and security. Yet through suffering, we can gain a closer relationship with God. When we suffer, we are permitted to share in the redemptive work of Jesus Christ. Our sufferings due to storms of any nature are to be offered to God as a sacrifice to better humanity and to bring peace to the world.

Postscript: After writing this testimony, Martha's husband, John, passed away in October 2020. His sudden passing brought a whole new set of challenges for Martha, which her deep faith is helping her get through. She greatly appreciates prayers.

Chapter 4

HOW WILL I LIVE WITHOUT HER?

This is the testimony of Bob Kaput about the impact of his wife's cancer.

On January 3, 2019, at 3:15 in the afternoon, only eight days after her sixty-sixth birthday and after seven plus months of increasingly intense suffering, my wife, Laurie, took her last breath and died. She had completed her earthly journey to her eternal destiny. Born into eternal life, she will suffer no more.

I also have suffered and am still suffering. Not only did Laurie suffer from her cancer, but I suffered with her each step of the way. From the devastating cancer diagnosis, through each failed chemo treatment, through multiple hospital stays, through the immunotherapy treatments which she was unable to complete, and through her ultimate final days and death, I suffered. And each family member suffered. Our friends also suffered with us.

I was raised in the 1950s culture that stressed that I, the husband, should protect my family from all evil, harm, and illness. In this case, I was powerless. And it hurt, it hurt deeply. There was nothing I could do to change the inevitable outcome—the death of my beloved Laurie.

This is our story, the story of Laurie and Bob, a story of growth in trust and faith in God in the face of intense suffering.

Our Childhood

Laurie was born the fourth of six siblings to an Irish father and Norwegian mother. There were eleven years between the third sibling, her only brother, and her. She was three years old when the first of her two younger sisters were born. She doted on them as if they were her children—an early indication of her concern for others.

She was raised a Catholic, and her family celebrated Mass every Sunday and on all holy days. Attending public schools, she regularly attended CCD classes and received the sacraments. Her family was very close, not only during her formative years, but throughout her life.

I, on the other hand, was the first of five siblings born to a first-generation Polish-American father and mother. We were raised Catholic, and our family—immediate and extended—was very close. After twelve years of Catholic schools and a two-year stint in the Marine Corps, I was ready to take on the world—ego and self-confidence were never an issue!

Our Marriage

We married young, especially by today's standards. A very, very brief chance encounter in a store parking lot is where we met. Laurie and her best friend at the time, someone that I knew, were leaving as I and my cousin arrived. A brief "Hi" between her best friend and me, an encounter that lasted all of fifteen seconds at most, was the extent of my first sight of Laurie.

Six months later, there was another very, very brief chance encounter, this one also lasting only a few seconds, at a different store, miles away, and one that I rarely frequented. We acknowledged each other as two who have seen each other previously but have never been introduced. At the time of this second "sighting" of Laurie, I still did not know her name. But even in the pre-internet days, there were ways to find out. Within days, I asked her out on a date. It was mid-December. Barely two months passed before we were engaged, and six months later, we were married—she was eighteen, I only four years her senior.

Just over nine months later, we became more than a wife and husband; we became a mother and father—a family! We quickly adapted to our new roles caring for our son and each other. Twenty-eight short months later, our first daughter was born. It had quickly become a family of four, and Laurie was not yet twenty-two. Thirteen years later, a big surprise resulted in our third child, another daughter.

We raised our three children teaching them the Catholic faith through word and, more importantly, through our actions—not always as smoothly as we should have. Our family celebrated Mass each Sunday and every holy day. We provided a nurturing environment, allowing our children to grow in faith, hope, and charity and providing them with an excellent life foundation that started them on their spiritual journey to the all-merciful God. They were loved and they knew it!

During our forty-seven plus years of marriage, our faith and trust in God grew as we were challenged several times. First, we had to leave our first child at the hospital. It was touch and go as to whether he would survive—a very difficult situation for a young mother and father. This son, during his teenage years, underwent successful chemo treatments for cancer. And we also had to deal with me, the primary bread winner, losing my job. In fact, looking back, I believe beyond a shadow of a doubt that these trials were preparing us for Laurie's upcoming ordeal, strengthening our faith and trust in God to face her upcoming devastating suffering.

Why Suffering?

Suffering is inevitable. From birth to death, we experience pain—psychological, physical, and spiritual. No exceptions! After all, God's own Son, Jesus, suffered extreme violence and a horrible death on the cross. And there was a divine purpose for this—it was the Son's unconditional love offering to the Father for our salvation in satisfaction for mankind's sins.

Why does God allow suffering? Briefly, God gave us free will and wants each of us to freely choose him for our eternal destiny. He does not force himself upon us. If he were to protect us from our choices that lead to suffering, his gift of a free will would be a sham and we would be incapable of choosing our eternal destiny.

So what possible good can come from suffering? Is it a wake-up call to reorient us on the path God wants us to choose? Maybe it is a catalyst for others to choose that same path leading to our and other's eternal salvation? Is it a call to transform us into the person God created? Or is it to deepen our faith and trust in God's mercy?

God does not force us on the path to him through our suffering. He merely allows the suffering so we can put our faith and trust in his love for us. And it is very important to realize that God can bring good out of any and all situations.

That good may impact the sufferer, those who observe the sufferer, and the world in general—all to bring about a closer relationship to God for the salvation of mankind. The more we grow in faith and trust in God and the more we lovingly serve God, the easier it is to face our suffering with complete trust in the all loving God. There is always a purpose to suffering; however, discovering that purpose may never be realized during a person's suffering or during a person's lifetime.

Laurie had experienced physical pain before, most notably in childbirth. We experienced psychological pain at the near death and later severe illness of our son. And she experienced spiritual pain when she had to come to grips with the death of her mother, father, and especially her brother. He was her only brother and he suffered greatly and wasted away from an aggressive cancer, dying at the young age of forty-three. She was devastated, the effect on her was dramatic. She knew that death is eventually inevitable, but she feared dying as her brother died—by wasting away. And like almost everyone, she hoped and prayed to not suffer as he did when it was her time to die. It was not to be.

Holy Spirit Prepares

Interestingly, in April 2018, I felt the urge to buy a book by Fr. Robert Spitzer on transforming suffering through faith. A few weeks later, in early May, I signed up for a Catholic Distance University seminar on why God allows suffering. These two events occurred even before Laurie was diagnosed with cancer.

Was this the Holy Spirit preparing me to assist Laurie through her upcoming health issues? We discussed this at length. It seemed as though God had a purpose in allowing her suffering. It was a real struggle trying to determine that purpose, trying to accept this new reality. We realized not only was her earthly life coming to an end but also that she may have to suffer as her brother did over thirty years ago—something she desperately wanted to avoid.

Her Suffering

Severe back pain she first noticed in December 2017 was diagnosed in late May as a rare form of stage four metastasized cancer. We were devastated! I had recently retired and we looked forward to spending much more time together. After the initial shock of this diagnosis, she was angry—angry since she never smoked, never even tried a cigarette, never tried illicit drugs, and for that matter, very rarely took any prescription drugs. Alcoholic beverages? Rarely. She just did not like the taste of beer, wine, and mixed drinks.

Why her she wondered? What was the purpose? Why not someone else? The struggle to understand was intense. We knew that our life together had changed—changed forever!

I struggled. Struggled as to why God would allow Laurie to suffer a fate similar to what her brother suffered. I have told many, many people over the years that my faith and trust in God has allowed me to accept the events that have come my way, such as my loss of a job during a severe recession, a child's serious illness and other challenging events. But this one was different, more critical, more life changing, more painful.

I prayed and prayed and prayed. Yes, for a cure, for I did not want to lose her. Yes, for relief from her increasingly intense suffering, so she would not suffer anymore. Yes, for the strength to be there for her as she needed. Her suffering caused me intense pain. Pain because I was unable to relieve her suffering. I would have traded places with her in a heartbeat, and I prayed for just that outcome, even though in comparison to her, I am a big baby when it comes to pain. All I could do was to be as supportive as possible, to help make Laurie's experience as tolerable as possible.

Were my prayers, and the prayers of all who said they would pray for us, answered? Well, there was no cure and we lost her to this devastating cancer. Prayers were answered though as she experienced some relief from the intensity of her suffering. Laurie did not undergo the severe side effects of that first chemo regime. The oncologist was very surprised. Everyone experienced somewhat intense side effects. There were side effects, for sure, but not as intense as the oncologist expected. We prayed that God would give us the strength to continue down the path of treatments hoping for positive results and for Laurie to stay strong enough to tolerate these treatments.

A question may arise as to exactly where was God in all this? Walking right beside us! We felt God's presence supporting us. We had a strong belief, a strong sense, that God shared our pain, shared our emotions, shared our distress. And our trust in God, in his mercy, grew much stronger during her ordeal.

Being a primary caregiver to a spouse with a terminal cancer illness is exceptionally stressful. In fact, primary caregivers experience various emotional, physical, and social issues that grow in degree the longer their spouse's illness and the greater their spouse suffers.

During the seven months of Laurie's cancer, I felt the presence of God supporting me to the extent that I felt almost no stress until the very last two weeks. Instead of stress overtaking me when I needed to be strong for her, to be present emotionally for her, my trust in God, trust that God is always with me, enabled me to go through her ordeal hand in hand with her. We both grew in that trust in God.

Our Spiritual Life Together

One day, midway through the disease process, her pain was very severe and getting worse, so I started a conversation with the question, "Do you know what you could do?" My intention was to encourage her to share with her friends and family the full extent, the severity, of her condition, as I knew they would provide even more support to her. Her reply to the question? "Yes, I should offer this to Jesus!"

I was surprised by her answer. Even though Laurie and I participated in Mass every Sunday, we did not pray together outside of sacramental Church celebrations. So I really did not know the extent of her prayer life, the depth of her spiritual life. However, since she was diagnosed with cancer, she told me numerous times that she was praying more frequently. She was more understanding of the faults of those around her (especially mine) and less stressed about things in general.

Yes, she was at times very stressed about the cancer, as was I, the all-too-frequent doctors' appointments, the treatments, but she was significantly calmer about it than anyone thought she would be. She had accepted her role, her suffering, just like Jesus did. Her attitude can only be attributed to the fact that she had become closer to God through her suffering.

On a chilly night, months before she died, we attended an Oktoberfest Party at a friend's residence. Even though she was struggling with her fate and in considerable pain, you would never guess it. She laughed and she listened to her friend's stories. Laurie answered those who asked about her treatments, always downplaying the severity of her condition and how she was dealing with it. She greatly enjoyed the party, as most of her friends were able to attend. It was for her an important time because she truly valued all her friends. And Laurie was a true inspiration to all those who attended the party. Her faith and trust in God were unmistakable and clearly evident. Her spirits were high after that party.

However, shortly after, we were devastated to find out that the second chemo treatment regimen, unfortunately, had not stopped the disease's progression. She was weak, weak from the physical and psychological stress of her condition. We once again had to address the question, what now? Our faith, our trust in God, even though somewhat shaken, pulled us through. We prayed with more passion that God would help us cope with this new reality. We prayed for all those affected by her death journey. She was mentally preparing for death. I, on the other hand, was not prepared for this eventuality.

Her Death

Seven days after entering the hospital, we celebrated her sixty-sixth birthday (December 26). The next day, she asked when our pastor would visit her. She was very, very weak. I told her that he was due there around noon. It was forty-five minutes past ten in the morning. I asked her if she could hold on until he came. Her reply? A not very convincing, "I think so!"

She was re-energized after our pastor's visit and receiving the sacrament of Anointing of the Sick. With her visiting family, however, we discussed routine topics unrelated to her cancer and her current condition. She wanted to go home—always a more comfortable place than a hospital—but she wanted enough of her strength to return first.

As the hours ticked by, her health was noticeably deteriorating. Our family took turns to ensure at least two were there to cover twenty-four hours a day sitting by her bedside in the hospital room. Laurie seemed to be mostly unresponsive. However, while some of us were talking with each other, Laurie would periodically add to the conversation—at the appropriate times and with appropriate comments. Surprisingly, she was still alert and engaged.

Later that same day, during a lull in the family con-versation, Laurie was heard speaking and she called out to her "mommy." When we asked her what she said, thinking that she was speaking to us, she told us that she was speaking "with people between the worlds." She was calm and appeared to be unafraid. On Friday, she entered the coma from which she would not recover.

It is said that people in a coma can hear and understand everything said in their presence. We trust that this is true, for Laurie was greatly loved by all of us. Each one of us spent time speaking alone with her, telling her how much she was loved, telling her how much she would be missed.

There is a well-known phenomenon which can get in the way of a person dying. Basically, the dying person needs to believe that when they die, their loved ones will be okay. Laurie lingered from Friday through her death the following Thursday, even though each day seemed most likely to be her last day. She lingered, in pain every time she was moved by the nursing staff, because of her concern for us, her love for us. She wanted to be 100 percent sure that we would be okay without her in dealing with life's challenges.

How It Affects Me Now

It has been almost seven months since Laurie died. How I wish she were still with me. My pain is very deep, my soul cries out in anguish every day. My struggle without her is still very difficult. Faith grown over seventy years has saved me from despair. Trust in God has been tested, severely tested, and has grown deeper through our suffering.

We had discussed dying long before her diagnosis— who would go first, how would the children cope, what should we do to prepare. These are typical for people our age to discuss, knowing that our mortal lives are nearing their end. As people of faith, we also discussed the after-life, relying on our Catholic knowledge and upbringing.

I am very unhappy that Laurie is gone. But I am very happy that she went first. Why? The answer is quite simple. I am glad that she was spared all the pain, the struggle, and the loneliness that I feel without her. I love her too much to have her go through what I am going through now.

My life-long spiritual journey to God has been quick-ening over the years, possibly the result of the aging pro-cess as I approach my inevitable death. It seems as though I make an ascent and then my journey hits a plateau, so to speak. What Laurie taught me through her ordeal, however, has affected me greatly.

Now, because of her very visible faith in God, my faith has been strengthened. Now, because of her very visible trust in God, my trust in God has soared. I am not afraid of suffering as Laurie suffered, although I am not in a hurry to suffer any more than I am currently suffering! I am not afraid of death, as Laurie died peacefully while I was stroking the hair on her head. Without a doubt in my being, I know that God was there comforting her and me when Laurie took her last breath.

People have told me that, with time, I will get over the death of Laurie. This is categorically incorrect! The reality is I will never "get over" her death. My pain of living without her penetrates to the core of my being and will remain forever. As I approach the seven-month anniversary of her birth into eternal life, I still hurt. My pain is still very intense, very deep. In a crowd of family and friends, I am lonely for her presence. I thank God daily for all the years we were together. There is no one with whom I would have wanted to share my life but my beloved Laurie!

So how do I cope? I pray that these emotions will soften in their intensity over time. I pray every single day, multiple times every day, for her, for my family, and for the strength to discern what God wants of me during my remaining years, as well as what God wanted me to learn from Laurie as she completed her earthly journey. My faith and trust in God grew significantly during this ordeal, and it sustains me now.

I did learn many things from her through her suffering, and these I will never forget. What I cherish, what really was impressive, what I will emulate, was her noticeable genuine concern for others throughout her life, which grew stronger during her increasingly intense pains and sufferings in her final seven months.

Her Legacy

How a person reacts to suffering is critical to that person's growth, that person's spiritual growth, for there is no growth more important. Laurie and I understood this better than many people. We knew she was in the last stages of her journey—a journey to eternal life with God for all eternity!

Acceptance of her disease, putting on a brave face, helping her family and friends deal with her inevitable demise, permeated her actions and her words. She did not want anyone to feel bad for her. She was thankful for all the support she was receiving from everyone and especially from me. And she suffered greatly watching me suffer, watching her cherished family suffer, watching her friends suffer because of her illness. It bothered her immensely.

So what is my perspective on Laurie's life and death? She, as all of us, was created by God to know, love, and serve God and God only. She, as all of us, was called by God by name to do his will. Having the God-given gift of a free will, she had a choice to make to determine her eternal destiny—that is, becoming God-centric or ego-centric.

She fulfilled his will being a loving daughter to her parents and a loving sister to her brother and sisters. She fulfilled his will being a loving, supportive, and dedicated wife. She fulfilled his will being a loving, nurturing mother and a loving, nurturing grandmother to her children and grandchildren. She fulfilled his will being a loving and supportive friend to so many. She fulfilled his will growing in love, kindness, charity, and compassion.

Laurie fulfilled God's purpose for her life. She chose a God-centric life. One can only speculate on what God's purpose for her suffering truly entailed. Maybe it was to bring all those who promised to pray for her closer to the all-merciful God. Maybe it was to provide a living example of how to have faith and trust in God when suffering. Maybe it was to purify her soul for union with the almighty and merciful God.

And these were some of her many accomplishments. Besides keeping me out of trouble (a major task in itself), she raised three exceptional Catholic children, positively impacted four grandchildren, and provided considerable support to her immediate and extended families. She was a major force with those she met, as evidenced by all the extraordinarily positive comments made by her friends and acquaintances.

Even now, so many months after her death, I have been told how she made others better people and how some regret not keeping in closer touch with her over the years. So many people offered to pray for her and our family, not only during her suffering, but also after her death. She clearly had a major impact on those who had the honor of meeting her and getting to know her.

Our children, their spouses, our grandchildren, and I are devastated by the loss of Laurie. Each one of us is struggling to deal with our grief. But Laurie's faith and trust in God, what she instilled in her family in words and in action, has given us the foundation to learn to live with the loss. Now, several months after Laurie's death, we feel God's presence and Laurie's presence in our lives.

Laurie mirrored Jesus's approach to suffering. She did not complain. She did not blame God. She offered her sufferings as her gift of love to God. She provided an incredibly powerful example of real faith and real trust in God. She accepted her sufferings and approaching death as a real Christian should—looking forward to participating in God's eternal life!

Yes, everyone misses her terribly—the struggle is still very real and the pain is still very deep. What we do going forward, inspired by her life, her suffering, her death, as an example of how we are to live and die, will be her life's legacy and God's ultimate purpose for her life.

Part II

SUFFERING CAUSED BY EVIL HUMAN BEHAVIOR

Chapter 5

WHY DOES GOD PERMIT MORAL EVIL?

We will next explore some reasons why a loving God might allow evil human behavior, which is called moral evil. Moral evil is, one way or another, the fault of humans, not nature. Moral evil includes specific acts of intentional wrongdoing, such as lying, stealing, raping, and murdering. Extreme examples of moral evil include Hitler's Auschwitz, Stalin's Gulags, and Pol Pot's killing fields in Cambodia.

We learn from the first chapters of the book of Genesis that God created a good world, a world where there was no moral evil or sin. However, it is important to realize that the potential for moral evil and sinful human behavior existed from the very beginning. That's because God created humans with the following characteristics:

- First, we are personal beings, capable of living relationships with our Creator and with our fellow human beings.
- Second, we are moral beings, with a

conscience that makes us aware of the difference between right and wrong. We praise, blame, counsel, and exhort each other. We do not hold machines morally responsible for what they do, no matter how complicated a machine.

- Third, we are rational beings, able to think, draw conclusions, and make sensible decisions, but also with the free will to make moral choices.

Our free will and rational nature are what makes humans in God's image and likeness. We are not puppets controlled by instinct, and we are not robots programmed to do whatever God dictates. Human beings without free will would be an animal or a machine. Instead, humans have the ability to obey God and the freedom to disobey him.

To have a free will means we are able to make voluntary choices. We do this every day. Moreover, the choices we make often reveal a direct link between suffering and human free will. That is because the freedom we have to make moral choices includes the possibility of making "bad" choices, which either intentionally or unintentionally harm ourselves or others. This could include ignoring the needs of our family or choosing lifestyle options that damage our physical, emotional, or spiritual health. It is the misuse of human free will, then, that is the "root cause" behind much of the moral evil and suffering we see in our world, in our communities, and in ourselves.

The Fall

Because God created human beings with a free will, it was up to us, not God, as to whether or not sin and moral evil would enter the world. God's plan had the potential for moral evil when God bestowed on human beings the gift of free will. Evil was inherent in God's risky gift of free will, but humans made it actual. As C. S. Lewis wrote in his book *The Problem of Pain*, "Christianity asserts that God is good; that He made all things good and for the sake of their goodness; that one of the good things He made, namely, the free will of rational creatures, by its very nature included the possibility of evil; and that creatures, availing themselves of this possibility, have become evil."[33]

The free will of the first man and woman (Adam and Eve) and humans ever since has been perverted by pride and disobedience. According to the Genesis creation story, Adam and Eve were enticed to "be like God" (Gn 3:5). The very first humans, through an act of free will, turned away from God and toward their own selfish desires. This prideful rebellion of our first parents against God is called the "original sin," and this resulted in "the Fall" of mankind into sin and caused evil and suffering to enter our world. As stated in the *Catechism of the Catholic Church*:

> Although set by God in a state of rectitude man, enticed by the evil one, abused his freedom at the very start of history. He lifted himself up against God and sought to attain his goal apart from him.

> By his sin Adam, as the first man, lost the original
> holiness and justice he had received from God, not
> only for himself but for all human beings. Adam
> and Eve transmitted to their descendants human
> nature wounded by their own first sin and hence
> deprived of original holiness and justice; this depri-
> vation is called "original sin." As a result of original
> sin, human nature is weakened in its powers, sub-
> ject to ignorance, suffering and the domination of
> death, and inclined to sin (this inclination is called
> "concupiscence"). (415–18)

The Fall of Adam and Eve both hurt themselves and
wounded human nature. In this sense, the "original sin"
could also be called the "original wound." St. Thomas
Aquinas explained how the Fall wounded human nature:

> Through the sin of our first parents, all the powers
> of the soul are left destitute of their proper order,
> whereby they are naturally directed to virtue. This
> destitution is called a wounding of nature.
>
> First, in so far as the reason, where prudence
> resides, is deprived of its order to the true, there is
> the wound of ignorance.
>
> Second, in so far as the will is deprived of its
> order to the good, there is the wound of malice.
>
> Third, in so far as the sensitive appetite is
> deprived of its order to the arduous, there is the
> wound of weakness.
>
> Fourth, in so far as it is deprived of its order to
> the delectable moderated by reason, there is the
> wound of concupiscence.

These four wounds, ignorance, malice, weakness
and concupiscence are afflicted on the whole of
human nature only as a result of our first parents'
sin.[34]

In other words, the first wound is blindness or ignorance, which is our loss of the intellectual capacity to
know and form proper judgments concerning spiritual
things.[35] The second wound, malice, is the result of our
will having lost the inclination to do good. The third
wound is weakness, which is the failure of our will to
develop a personal offense against evil. Finally, the fourth
wound is concupiscence, which is the disordered desire
for immediate sensual gratification. These wounds of our
human nature diminished the gifts of God to Adam and
Eve of original justice, integrity, immortality, and infused
knowledge and make it more difficult for each of us to
pursue true happiness.[36]

In short, we humans, through misuse of our free will
in generation after generation, have gotten ourselves into
an impossible bind. Sin has wrecked us in such a fundamental way that we and our societies have become dys-
functional. This is the fundamental reason why there is
so much suffering and moral evil in our world.

The Fall and Science

The *Catechism of the Catholic Church* (CCC) also makes
clear that even though the story of the Fall in Genesis uses
symbolic and figurative language (e.g., a talking snake),
it describes a real event that occurred at the beginning

of human history. For example, CCC 390 on "How to Read the Account of the Fall," affirms the following: "The account of the fall in Genesis 3 uses figurative language, but affirms a primeval event, a deed that took place at the beginning of the history of man. Revelation gives us the certainty of faith that the whole of human history is marked by the original fault freely committed by our first parents."

Moreover, the reality of the original sin and the Fall of the first man and first woman is true even if scientists confirm that the physical body of human beings emerged from a relatively large humanoid population of common genetic lineage rather than from a single pair of homo sapiens.[37] Since human beings are an integral unity of body *and* soul, the first truly human man and the first truly human woman could have been created when God imparted a soul into their preexistent physical body, even if their bodies had evolved from lower life forms over very long periods of time.[38]

As stated by Pope St. John Paul II, "It is possible that the human body, following the order impressed by the Creator on the energies of life, could have been gradually prepared in the forms of antecedent living beings. However, the human soul, on which man's humanity definitively depends, cannot emerge from matter, since the soul is of a spiritual nature."[39]

Only these first two people with a soul (Adam and Eve) would have been truly human—body and soul together.[40] The Catechism states:

The human body shares in the dignity of "the image of God": it is a human body precisely because it is animated by a spiritual soul, and it is the whole human person that is intended to become, in the body of Christ, a temple of the Spirit: "Man, though made of body and soul, is a unity. Through his very bodily condition he sums up in himself the elements of the material world. Through him they are thus brought to their highest perfection and can raise their voice in praise freely given to the Creator. For this reason man may not despise his bodily life. Rather he is obliged to regard his body as good and to hold it in honor since God has created it and will raise it up on the last day."

The Church teaches that every spiritual soul is created immediately by God—it is not "produced" by the parents—and also that it is immortal: it does not perish when it separates from the body at death, and it will be reunited with the body at the final Resurrection. (364, 366)

The Fall and Suffering

The Bible and the Church also teach the divine revelation that death, evil, and suffering entered the world through the Fall of Adam and Eve. Genesis makes this point:

> To the woman he said, "I will greatly multiply your pain in childbearing; in pain you shall bring forth children, yet your desire shall be for your husband, and he shall rule over you."

And to Adam he said, "Because you have listened
to the voice of your wife, and have eaten of the tree
of which I commanded you, 'You shall not eat of
it,' cursed is the ground because of you; in toil you
shall eat of it all the days of your life; thorns and
thistles it shall bring forth to you; and you shall eat
the plants of the field. In the sweat of your face you
shall eat bread till you return to the ground, for out
of it you were taken; you are dust, and to dust you
shall return." (3:16–19)

The *Catechism* also affirms:

Scripture portrays the tragic consequences of this
first disobedience. Adam and Eve immediately lose
the grace of original holiness. They become afraid
of the God of whom they have conceived a distorted
image—that of a God jealous of his prerogatives.

The harmony in which they had found themselves, thanks to original justice, is now destroyed:
the control of the soul's spiritual faculties over the
body is shattered; the union of man and woman
becomes subject to tensions, their relations
henceforth marked by lust and domination. Harmony with creation is broken: visible creation has
become alien and hostile to man. Because of man,
creation is now subject "to its bondage to decay."
Finally, the consequence explicitly foretold for this
disobedience will come true: man will "return to
the ground", for out of it he was taken. Death makes
its entrance into human history. (399–400)

And St. Paul teaches, "Therefore as sin came into the world through one man and death through sin, and so death spread to all men because all men sinned" (Rom 5:12). Of course, there had been a lot of physical death throughout the long evolutionary process and development of life on earth. However, spiritual death is clearly of a more serious consequence than physical death. Thus, we can interpret the death wrought by original sin as a spiritual death resulting in loss of eternal life in heaven (at least until the redemption brought by Jesus Christ).

Dr. Peter Kreeft and Fr. Ronald Tacelli present three ways that the original sin of our first parents could have brought about the moral evil and natural evil we experience in the world today:

> The first and simplest is that the "thorns and this-tles" were there before the Fall but they only hurt afterward. The second is that fallen angels had already corrupted the earth, but God protected Adam and Eve in a special garden; they abandoned this protection when they abandoned God the protector. (This theory was held by some of the Church Fathers; we wonder whether there is any good theological or scientific disproof of it or if it is just unfashionable to take seriously the work of demons.) The third is that Adam was the priest of the world, and the Fall was like saying a Black Mass, perverting everything. The bottom line is, of course, that we do not know and can only speculate about how it happened.[41]

Fr. Daniel has some interesting insights in a blog regarding the concern expressed above that today it is often not fashionable to take seriously that the devil, demons, and fallen angels are real and that hell really exists:

> Careful analysis of recent studies and polls taken among Catholics reveals that an overwhelming majority of U.S. Catholics simply do not believe in the Devil, or sin, or it's logical consequences—eternal damnation in hell.
>
> Jesus Christ told us plainly in scriptures that hell was created "for the devil and his angels." But if these persons are symbolic, does that mean hell is too? And if hell is symbolic, why wouldn't heaven also be symbolic? The two are intimately related to each other, as we come to understand when we study "The Four Last Things."
>
> The other consequence if there is no hell, then there is no justice, and if there is no justice there is no God. This would also mean that if there is no justice, then humanity does not possess free will. For justice is the natural end of free will, that individuals at the end of their life are given what they deserve, their due.[42]

Whether fashionable or not, Jesus's struggle against demons and the powers of evil is quite evident in the Gospel narratives. The Church has long held that these powers and principalities are real forces that stand behind much of the evil in the world. Pope Francis reinforced this Church teaching in his apostolic exhortation

Gaudete Et Exsultate (*On The Call To Holiness In Today's World*), "We should not think of the devil as a myth, a representation, a symbol, a figure of speech or an idea. This mistake would lead us to let down our guard, to grow careless and end up more vulnerable. The devil does not need to possess us. He poisons us with the venom of hatred, desolation, envy and vice. When we let down our guard, he takes advantage of it to destroy our lives, our families and our communities."[43]

We are not only physical beings, we are also spiritual beings. Whether we acknowledge it or not, we are subject to the suggestions and impressions of other spiritual beings—notably a Holy Spirit that loves us and is calling us to eternal love and other evil spirits that do not love us and are trying to bring us into their own narcissism and darkness.[44]

In his book *Mere Christianity*, C. S. Lewis wrote of a dark power in the universe, the driving force behind death, disease, and sin. This universe is at war, he writes. It is not a war between independent powers, but rather a civil war, a rebellion. And we are living in the part of the universe occupied by the rebel. He writes, "Enemy-occupied territory—that is what this world is. Christianity is the story of how the rightful king has landed, you might say landed in disguise, and is calling us all to take part in a great campaign of sabotage."[45]

The Church and C. S. Lewis are right. We are under occupation by a dark and malevolent army, with Satan at the helm. We can't directly see him and his minions because they operate mainly in a different realm—a dimension from which they can see us and influence our minds. They've successfully spread death, disease, and sin among us. In fact, they're so good at influencing mankind that they've fooled many of us into thinking they don't even exist, enabling them to carry out their evil deeds with even greater impunity. Their ultimate objective is to delude and mislead humans so that we die in a poor spiritual state and thus become Satan's victim and slave for all eternity.

So how do we follow the lead of our rightful king—Jesus Christ—and carry out "acts of sabotage" against our occupiers, in order to thwart their agenda in the here and now, and avoid becoming their eternal slave and victim in the hereafter? To protect ourselves against the influences of evil and instead be guided by God's love and goodness, we need to pray regularly, practice moral living, prayerfully reflect on the Scriptures, and be active in a church community, including regularly obtaining God's power and grace in the sacraments—especially confession and the Eucharist. Even with these four life-habits, we are vulnerable to incursion by evil and a tendency to resist obeying God's will for our lives; without them, we are virtually defenseless.[46]

It is important, however, to remember our own culpability due to our pride and self-centeredness in choosing to do what we want instead of seeking what God wants in our lives. Mankind's initial and continuing rebellion against God is the source of moral evil and sin in our world. As stated by C. S. Lewis, "From the moment a creature [human being] becomes aware of God as God and of itself as self, the terrible alternative of choosing God or self for the center is opened to it. This sin is committed daily by young children and ignorant peasants as well as by sophisticated persons, by solitaries no less than by those who live in society: it is the fall in every individual life, and in each day of each individual life, the basic sin behind all particular sins."[47]

The Ongoing Consequences of the Fall

The Church also teaches that all people today and throughout history suffer the consequences of the sins of our first parents and of humans ever since. No one is immune from the pain and suffering caused by sin.[48] The *Catechism* explains:

> All men are implicated in Adam's sin, as St. Paul affirms: "By one man's disobedience many (that is, all men) were made sinners": "sin came into the world through one man and death through sin, and so death spread to all men because all men sinned."
> . . .
> Following St. Paul, the Church has always taught that the overwhelming misery which oppresses men and their inclination towards evil and death cannot be understood apart from their connection with Adam's sin and the fact that he has transmitted to us a sin with which we are all born afflicted, a sin which is the "death of the soul." . . .
> How did the sin of Adam become the sin of all his descendants? The whole human race is in Adam "as one body of one man." By this "unity of the human race" all men are implicated in Adam's

sin, as all are implicated in Christ's justice. Still, the transmission of original sin is a mystery that we cannot fully understand. But we do know by Revelation that Adam had received original holiness and justice not for himself alone, but for all human nature. By yielding to the tempter, Adam and Eve committed a personal sin, but this sin affected the human nature that they would then transmit in a fallen state. It is a sin which will be transmitted by propagation to all mankind, that is, by the transmission of a human nature deprived of original holiness and justice. And that is why original sin is called "sin" only in an analogical sense: it is a sin "contracted" and not "committed"—a state and not an act. (402–4)

All of us, ever since Adam and Eve, have to one degree or another bought into Satan's lie that we can "be like God." At the heart of this lie that we see in the Genesis account is the deification of the ego. I become the center of the universe—I with all my wants, my fears, and my demands. And when I am the center of the cosmos, the basic reality between humans all too easily becomes one of rivalry, competition, violence, and mistrust—giving rise to the moral evil that we see in the world today and throughout human history. Thus both sin and suffering in the world are traceable to the free will of mankind, not to God.

WHY DOES GOD PERMIT MORAL EVIL?   97

Why Do We Have Free Will?

All this leads to a profoundly important question; namely, why did God give humans free will and then allow us to misuse it? Why should God have taken such an obvious risk in giving human beings a free will in the first place?

We have free will because God wants each of us to *voluntarily choose* to know, love, and serve him (see CCC 1721). Real love—our love of God and our love of each other—must involve a free choice. True love is totally voluntary. It cannot be forced.

Fr. Robert Spitzer has this to say about true love:

> If one does not have the freedom to choose unloving behaviors, then one's loving behaviors are not really chosen—they are merely programmed (like impulses, desires, or instincts). Beings which have no real alternatives are not the true initiators of their actions; they are merely responding to stimuli in the only way they can. Thus, if one's love is not chosen, one's love is not one's own. It originates from a cause other than one's self.
>
> Love, which is not one's own, is not love at all. It is merely programmed behaviors for the purpose of producing beneficial effects. Computers can be programmed to do very positive and beneficial actions (and programmed not to do negative actions), but we certainly would not say that those computers are loving.
>
> God's dilemma now becomes apparent. If God is to create a loving being, He must create that being

with the capacity to create a loving action anew; and if He is to create a being with that capacity, He must create a being with the capacity to choose love or unlove; and if He creates a being with that capacity, He creates the very possibility of unlove leading to suffering.[49]

True love, therefore, proceeds only from a free choice. A free choice, however, leaves the possibility of a wrong choice. With God granting humans a free will came the possibility that people might instead choose to hate—not love—God and each other. Think about how important our free will must be to God, since God created people who could use the gift of freedom to hurt others and even hate God himself.

British author and mystic Caryll Houselander wrote the following particularly insightful reflection on this topic:

Suppose that God gave every person the choice between a world in which there was no suffering, but also no capacity for love, or a world in which suffering remains, but everyone has the power to love. Which do you think mankind would choose? Which would you choose? Quite certainly the power to love, even at the cost of suffering. Now this is precisely what has happened. The thing which makes us able to love is free-will, and it is the same thing, free-will, which makes us able to sin. Without it there would be no sin and no love in the world. Suffering is the result of sin. . . . God does all he can to change suffering from something that crushes and destroys us into something that exalts and renews us. This is a miracle which could be effected only by absolute love and beside which the creation of the world is pale.[50]

Not even an all-powerful God could give humans a free will while guaranteeing that we would always use it wisely. That's because God could not prevent moral evil without removing our freedom. Not even God can bestow and withhold freedom at the same time. A person who is genuinely free and yet not free is a logical contradiction. Our free will must include the possibility of sin and moral evil. God did his part perfectly; we humans are the ones who messed it up.

Free Will and Heaven

This discussion of free will also leads to an interesting question. Since we have free will on earth, it seems likely that we will also have free will in heaven. But since the beginning of human history, people have used their free will to choose sin and evil. Therefore, how can we have free will in heaven, yet heaven still be without sin and moral evil? In other words, how would heaven be any different from earth?

It seems the answer is that the only people in heaven are those who, by the grace of God, are capable of fully aligning their own free will with God's will and doing only the good (not sin). For as Jesus taught us to pray in the Lord's Prayer, "Thy will be done on earth as it is in heaven." By these words, Jesus showed how important it is for us to follow the will of God on earth. He also implied by these words that God's will is perfectly followed in heaven.

As St. Anselm wrote, "No one will have any other desire in heaven than what God wills; and the desire of one will be the desire of all; and the desire of all and of each one will also be the desire of God."[51] Thus, we must be able and willing to do only the will of God when in heaven.

In order to be with God in heaven, therefore, we need to be perfect as God is perfect. For as Jesus said, "You, therefore, must be perfect, as your heavenly Father is perfect" (Mt 5:48). We know this is true because God has predestined us for one thing—heaven—where all is perfect and everyone is without sin. For as Scripture states, "But nothing unclean shall enter it, nor any one who practices abomination or falsehood" (Rv 21:27).

Anyone who has not been completely freed from the tendency to sin is, to some extent, "unclean." Through repentance, we gain the grace needed to be worthy of heaven. But while we have been forgiven and our soul is spiritually alive, this alone is not sufficient for gaining entrance into heaven.

All Christians agree that nobody will sin in heaven. Therefore, we need to be completely cleansed of our sinful tendencies before we can enter heaven. Sin and the final glorification in heaven are utterly incompatible. As Pope Benedict XVI stated, "God is so pure and holy that a soul stained by sin cannot be in the presence of the divine majesty."[52] Thus, it follows that people are unlikely to enter heaven until they are fully willing and able to not sin.

In other words, without the gift and grace of perfect holiness, which is possible only when we actively cooperate with the power and presence of the Holy Spirit in our lives, we cannot be with God in heaven. Sanctification is the grace-filled process by which we become holy.

This perfection of holiness is not an option. It is not something that may or may not happen before we get into heaven. It is an absolute requirement. As Hebrews 12:14 states, we must strive "for that holiness without which no one will see the Lord."

Therefore, we need to make a serious effort to deepen our union with God and grow in personal holiness while here on earth. Only when we die to our selfish and sinful desires and achieve perfect union with Christ will we be holy and perfect. Of course, we cannot do this just by ourselves. Rather, we are to humbly act in complete cooperation with the grace and power of God in our lives, especially through the sacraments of the Church.

Even though we have been saved by Christ's passion and death on the cross, we will not be able to enter heaven until we are fully able and willing not to sin and have learned how to completely align our will with God's will. This helps explain why growth in virtue and holiness should be a primary purpose in our life. This will be discussed later in this book, including how suffering often provides the means by which we are able to grow in holiness.

Avoiding Tyrannical Behavior

However, until we attain the gift of perfect holiness, and given our fallen human nature, we are all capable of dark and evil acts. As such, could much of the moral evil in the world be caused by people who are trying to feel good about themselves by feeling superior to others?

We see this in bullying, insulting others, putting them down, and belittling gossip, as well as in the many horrific crimes and wars throughout history. This certainly does not mean such tyrannical behavior is justified. But understanding why this evil, domineering, and even murderous behavior can occur may help reduce its likelihood.

It is a well-known fact that many tyrants in history, including Adolf Hitler, Josef Stalin, Mao Zedong, and Saddam Hussein, had a deprived childhood devoid of love and acceptance.[53] Nearly all were brutally beaten as a matter of course during their childhood. Many people, not just murderous dictators, who are emotionally deprived and physically abused during childhood may subconsciously develop ego-defense mechanisms and behaviors to compensate for their poor self-image.

John Powell states in his classic bestselling book *Why Am I Afraid to Tell You Who I Am?*, "The Dominator is often characterized by an exaggerated desire to control the lives of others as well as their thought processes. Like most people who exaggerate their importance or wisdom, dominators are bothered by subconscious feeling of inadequacy. It is strange that very often such people are so determined to feel adequate that they are distracted from the fact of their domineering ways. They usually explain their domination as necessary, reasonable and justifiable. Dominators are very often troubled by feelings of hostility."[54]

Domineering and tyrannical behavior in both children and later as adults can be avoided if parents do their best to make sure each of their children *feel* their deep and unconditional love. It is not enough for children to know that their parents love them. Each child must feel it. They have to be certain, deep down in their innermost being, of their parent's unconditional love and acceptance.

Through all the ups and downs, joys and disappointments, and good and bad choices in life, children need to know that they do not have to earn their parents' love, nor can they ever lose it. Of course, parents should not approve of or encourage bad behavior. However, parents can guide their children along right paths without withholding their love or making it conditional upon their child's behavior.

Mature Christians, moreover, know they do not need to feel superior to or dominate others to feel good about themselves, no matter how wounded they may have been as a child. That's because our Christian identity is grounded in the realization that each one of us is a gifted child of a loving and merciful God (see 1 Jn 3:1). God's love for us does not depend on what we do or don't do. God loves us unconditionally and no sin, no failing, no weakness can keep God from loving each of us like there is only one of us to love.[55]

God's deep and permanent love for each of us is even greater than the love of a mother for her child and the love of a lover who gives all for his beloved. *The deepest need in the human heart is to know we are loved, and Christians recognize that we are deeply loved by the God of the universe.* Catholic author Don Schwager addresses this in a daily Scripture meditation:

> Jesus on many occasions spoke to his disciples about the nature of God's unquenchable love. *God is love* (1 John 4:16) because He is the creator and source of all that is true love. His love is unconditional, unmerited, and unlimited. We can't buy it, earn it, demand it. It is a pure gift, freely given, and freely received. God's love doesn't change or waver. It endures because it is eternal and timeless. It's the beginning and the end—the purpose for which God created us and why He wants us to be united with Him in a bond of unbreakable love. And it's the essence of what it means to be a son or daughter of God the eternal Father.[56]

The realization of how deeply God loves us enables Christians to overcome burdens of inferiority, inadequacy, or low self-esteem by helping us realize that our worth and value does not come from how we look, how talented we are, what we do, or what people say about us. Rather, we are valuable because of who made us. We are each God's creation and are made in the image and likeness of God (see Gn 1:26–27). Our value, therefore, comes directly from God and our worth goes well beyond our looks, abilities, or achievements. As shared by Ashley Oliver, a contributor to *The Upper Room*:

When I was a freshman in high school, I was diagnosed with an eating disorder. For over two years, I despised my body. In this state it was impossible for me to believe that I had been created in God's image or that God loved me the way I was. When I finally began my journey to recovery, I slowly began to understand that everyone has been created in God's perfect image. Through the years, I have learned that every single thing that God created is beautiful and wonderful, including each of us. Regardless of the flaws we see in ourselves, God doesn't make mistakes. The way we are is the way God intended us to be. So as we go through life, we try to remember that God loves us exactly as we are. God's works are wonderful; and God loves and accepts us, flaws and all. With God's help, we can love ourselves and others as God loves us.[57]

While devout Christians constantly strive with God's help to become better persons, we are able to accept the self-worth and dignity that come from being a beloved child of an all-loving and all-knowing God. As children of God, we can abandon the need to compare ourselves with others and hold onto the truth that each of us has been blessed with the individual talents and unique gifts that God has chosen to give us. This awareness helps Christians accept and love who we are, especially when we also realize that *God doesn't make junk.*[58]

In this chapter, we explored why suffering is an inevitable part of our fallen world.[59] Because of our fallen human nature, our bodies move inexorably towards death and the sufferings that precede it. Everyone suffers. How we respond to our suffering makes all the difference, as we have been discovering though the stories shared in this book, including those that follow.

Chapter 6

MAN'S INHUMANITY TO MAN

This is the testimony of Richard McLeon about his experiences during the Gulf War and his family's struggles after the sudden and unexpected loss of his job.

"Is there a Staff Sergeant McLeon here?"

The teaching assistant scanned the room as I slowly raised my hand. I was beginning my graduate studies—in my first semester—when Iraq invaded the tiny nation of Kuwait. I had been a US Army Reserve Nuclear, Biological, and Chemical (NBC) Specialist for almost eight years.

Patty and I had been married for less than two years, and although both of us were baptized Christians and firm in our faith in Jesus, we had not found a church home. We were raised in different denominations, and despite trying for over a year to find a church, we had finally given up and simply quit attending.

We had decided to quit our jobs and move to College Station, Texas, where I could begin graduate studies and Patty could continue working towards her bachelor's degree. We had a plan.

There is an old Yiddish saying that goes *Mann tracht, Un Gott lacht,* "Man plans, and God laughs."

We had a plan.

Unfortunately, our plan did not foresee Saddam Hussein ordering the invasion of Kuwait. As a US Army Reserves Nuclear, Biological, and Chemical Senior Instructor, I had delivered numerous threat briefings on the Iraqi's chemical warfare capabilities and the prolific use of chemical and toxic agents during the Iran-Iraq War.

The commitment of US forces to the Kingdom of Saudi Arabia and the news that the US Reserve forces would be needed was ominous. Patty and I knew how small the US Army Chemical Corps was and that the chances of me getting called up were better than average.

That call found me in a college classroom in early September 1990.

But dear Lord, Patty and I have a plan.

Our plan was to put our lives on hold for a few years: Patty would finish her bachelor's degree and I would finish my master's. Then we would return to the workforce, start our family, and have successful careers.

Now the political and economic ambition of one person on the other side of the world had the effect of throwing our plans to the wind. It just wasn't right, and it wasn't fair. Where was justice? Our world was being thrown aside and we were being torn apart for an indefinite time. The rumors were rampant that we would be overseas for two years. That Patty and I would not see each other for two long years. We tried not to think about or talk about the injustice of it all, but how could God let this happen? What had we done to deserve this?

Within forty-eight hours we celebrated our second anniversary three months early and said good-bye for now as I reported for active duty at Ft. Polk, Louisiana. Then it was on to ad-Dammam, Saudi Arabia, where our US Army Reserve Chemical Company was assigned to the XVIII Airborne Corps and attached to the 24th Infantry Division (Mechanized).

I found myself in the northern desert of the Kingdom of Saudi Arabia. If you had been there with us, in that place, you would know that there is no reason to say that it was hot. It was always hot.

We existed on a small patch of real estate that consisted of sand and volcanic rock. My "home" was an eight foot by eight foot hole in the ground about one thousand meters south of the western tip of the neutral zone between northern Saudi Arabia and Iraq. The Iraqi Army was three thousand meters away, across the border and across the mine fields that we came to know all too well.

In 1990, they were the fifth largest army in the world and had combat experience, fighting a seven-year war with Iran to the east. Only a few of us had any sort of combat experience at all. We were young, inexperienced, and afraid. We woke up every morning within range of the same Soviet-made rockets that they had so often fired into Iran.

We sat there in the northern Arabian Desert for months. We knew that a fight was coming—and that death awaited some of us. That calm before the battle can be the worst part.

Our mission was chemical reconnaissance and decontamination. Most troops were under-trained in NBC (Nuclear, Biological, Chemical) Operations and we barely had enough decontamination equipment to save ourselves, much less the entire 24th Infantry Division.

You question everything in your fear and in your boredom. Depression, anger, and insecurity creep in and remind you of all your failures. Jealousy whispers in your ear that those you love at home are doing just fine without you, making new friends and getting on with their life—without you.

You feel like you have lost everything and that you are living on a pendulum that swings between your heart telling you it's going to be okay and your mind telling you that all hope is lost.

I missed Patty with all my heart, and I was angry. Angry that I didn't have the equipment I needed, angry that I was a world away from my wife, and angry that we had uprooted our lives to follow our plan. It was a good plan.

One day, an Army chaplain wandered into our midst. I don't remember his name, and frankly, I don't think that he would have wanted me to. This humble servant of God had been called not to bring himself to us but to bring us to the Lord.

He began with a simple Bible study on the side of a sand dune. There were no stained-glass windows, no pews, no bells, no statutes, and no choir. Yet, in the midst of our fear, we heard the Shepherd's voice and we found hope, and in that impossibly desperate situation, we found joy.

Prayer re-entered my life and I found the strength and the peace that only God can provide.

Our "congregation" slowly grew, and one day, as we were walking to meet the chaplain, another soldier came slowly toward us. He quietly asked me if he could join us and stated that although he couldn't explain it, he felt drawn to be with us.

He said, "Back in the world, I'm successful, I've got everything I want: but none of that stuff is doing me any good right now. I want to know, I need to know, what you guys know."

We explained that the question wasn't "what we know" but "who we know."

He started coming with us and I realized that I had been blessed to witness the Shepherd calling to his own and to rejoice with the angels as another lost lamb came into the fold. Hope was restored.

A month or two passed and we found ourselves at the point of the spear. My platoon was charging a phase line deep into Iraq with the 24th Infantry (M). We were nestled between the tanks and mechanized infantry before us and the artillery behind us. Tanks equipped with bulldozer blades lead the charge with their blades cutting a path through the desert and pushing aside thousands of rounds of unexploded US ordinance dropped during the six weeks of air war.

They created a two or three lane highway with a three-foot shoulder that may, or may not, contain the explosive remnants of Operation Desert Shield. To veer into the shoulder was to risk your life and those of your troops. We drove for days through mine fields, enemy troops, and an endless open desert. Unfortunately, my driver was night blind, so I supervised my troops by day and drove all night.

Somewhere, somebody in the Army had made the command decision that our platoon did not need night vision goggles. That meant that we were driving sixty mph across the open desert in blackout conditions, sand billowing up from the armor and mechanized infantry in front of us, potentially explosive shoulders on either side of the "road," and very little visibility to see where we were going at night.

Typically, the moon would shine enough to give me about fifteen feet of visibility through the blowing sand. That often allowed me to see the rear of the vehicle in front of me, but sometimes it was so thick that I couldn't see the end of the hood of my five-ton truck.

I was driving all night, every night, and leading and securing my troops every day. After a few days, the adrenaline was fading and I was simply exhausted. Death was all around us and the stress of combat, leadership, and a severe lack of sleep started to take their toll.

Somewhere in the open desert that night I was pushed to my limit. I had been awake for most of three days, was exhausted, and the sand was so thick that I had lost sight of the vehicle in front of me. I could feel the right front tire of my vehicle begin to climb the shoulder again and I swerved left. I slowed down hoping that the sand would settle, but there was no relief.

I felt like the world was closing in all around me. Pressures, stresses, were suffocating me. I felt like I was drowning in a deep pool of despair with no way out.

Worse still, my failure would bring down my platoon. Those soldiers were counting on me, and I was slowly fading, slipping away. I can't explain it if you haven't been there, but a person knows, instinctively, when you are at the end of your capacity. I was there. I was ready to stop the vehicle and simply walk away.

In that moment, I prayed.

I prayed that God would help me. I prayed, "Father, I know that in your Word it states that you will never give us more than we can handle. I know that you know all that is in my heart and in my mind and I know that you know that I am at my breaking point and death is at my door. Father, I just can't handle any more and I beg you for your help. Please, Father, in the name of your son Jesus Christ, please, please help me. Amen."

As I said "Amen," I sat there exhausted, broken, and empty, ready to simply park the five-ton truck and walk away. That was when I saw the first dark spot on the hood of the truck. It was followed by another and another. Tears came down my face as I realized that God had heard my prayer and was sending a light rain to settle the sand and to refresh my soul.

The rain was just enough to energize me to keep moving. As the sand and dust settled, I realized that the convoy had pulled off some fifty yards ahead of me. The tears of awe and thanks ran down my face as I rejoined the safety of the convoy. I knew that God had heard my prayer and I knew that he had not abandoned me in my weakest hour. I had reached out to God and he had reached out to me, just like the Church had told me he would many, many years before. I knew that God is still alive.

I have noticed this familiar and comforting pattern many times over the years. We find ourselves in desperate situations, some of our doing, some not. Sometimes we just make mistakes and people get hurt. Sometimes we make mistakes and hurt ourselves. We are blessed with a loving God that is full of grace and offers forgiveness and healing when we stumble and fall. We only need to open our hearts to him and accept the forgiveness offered through the sacrifice of our Lord, Jesus.

Peace and healing are a sincere prayer away.

It would be difficult to say that the Gulf War was a good experience. In many ways, the things I've seen and heard and smelled on the Highway of Death still haunt me. But I cannot say that it was a bad experience either.

As a result of the war, Patty and I both returned to prayer and to the Church. We saw God take a terrible situation and craft it into something that drew us closer together, and closer to him. Upon my return from southwest Asia, we immediately rededicated ourselves to God, began searching for a church family, and we have continued worshipping together ever since.

I have come to understand most of life's ups and downs as being the product of free will in a fallen world.

Like Hitler, Saddam acted out of his own free will. He chose to invade Kuwait and, like dominoes standing in a row, his actions affected millions of people; tens of thousands suffered and died. We ask God, "How could you let this happen? How can you allow one person's action to hurt so many? Where is justice?"

Over the years, I have also come to understand that God is infinitely loving and generous. It is his nature to open his arms and to offer his love and his gifts to all his children. Free will, like God's love and salvation, is freely offered to everyone. God, in his infinitely just nature, doesn't discriminate between us but offers his riches to all his children. Some use his gifts to help others, some use the gifts to help themselves. It is ultimately up to each of us to decide how we will use the gift of free will.

Every family has generous, loving members. Someone who would share anything they have with you and offer unconditional love. Likewise, every family has selfish, rebellious members: those who will say and do anything to take things like joy, love, and peace away from you. Why should all of humanity be any different?

Sometimes people simply exert their free will in ways that hurt others.

God does not take his gift away from his children simply because someone abused it. Instead, he wisely waits for our reaction. How will we respond when someone's free will gets in the way of our happiness? Will we rail against God or will we turn to him for help? Will we stay in the mud and muck and plan our revenge, or will we turn to God and ask him to help us and those that are lost?

Thankfully, our Creator knows us better than we know ourselves and understands that sometimes situations not of our control push us to our limits.

Sudden Job Loss

After the war, Patty and I completed our degrees and started our family. I had made a career in the non-profit world and was ordained as a priest serving the Anglican Church in bi-vocational ministry. We had a little farm in the Piney Woods of Texas and had wonderful Christian friends nearby. Things were going great: our sons were maturing into fine men, the bills were paid, and we were beginning to think about retirement.

Our sons are Texas National Guard Infantrymen and found themselves deployed to the Horn of Africa. Their cards and phone calls told us about the great suffering of the people in that region of Africa. We expanded our prayer and donation list, all the time keeping an expectant eye on retirement.

We had a plan. God laughed.

My non-profit, secular employer fired me for "no cause" after six and a half years as its general manager. The board of directors began and concluded their deliberations with a 4-3 split board.

I asked, "What have I done wrong?" I was told, "Nothing." I asked, "What have I not done that you've asked me to do?" Again, I was told, "Nothing." I was confused—every financial and managerial metric of the company had improved under my watch. This should not be happening!

I wanted to argue with them, to demand an explanation, to face the root cause of this injustice and evil, but in my mind, I heard, ". . . like a sheep being led to slaughter . . . , he was silent." Silence is not one of my best traits, so again, I mustered my thoughts and prepared my defense. Again, I heard the words of Isaiah, and Matthew, Luke, Mark, and John: "and he was silent."

Patty and I had a mortgage, car payments, and two sons in college. I had six years of employee evaluations marked "Exceeds Expectations." This cannot be happening.

I was mad. I was angry. I was hurt. But again, I was guided by the Holy Spirit and remained silent.

Nothing was offered other than, "We think that it's time to change directions." Many employees came to my defense to no avail. Later I was told the event was the result of small-town politics and had nothing to do with my performance. The board that had hired me had rotated out and a new board was in majority.

Sometimes I think that it would have been easier if I had done something wrong. Then I could at least point to some weakness, some flaw that needed correcting. Instead I was faced with the absolute injustice of being fired "without cause."

I was mad. I was angry. I was hurt. I felt like I had let my family down. I felt like I had let my employees down.

This forced my family to live in a storm where our faith was shaken, and our very financial stability was questionable. We asked, "Where is justice?" and "How can God let this happen?" "How can evil win like this?" We cried out, "Why Lord? Why did this happen?" We were injured and hurting through no fault of our own, victims of small minds, ignorance, and small-town politics.

I had never been fired in my life, and I certainly never thought it would happen for doing a good job. The injustice of it was always on my mind. How can people just throw my family away and inflict that kind of hurt and pain without a second thought? It was a bitter pill and we suffered through months of depression, sleepless nights, hurt, self-doubt, and the general trials of unemployment.

Why was God silent? Why wasn't he moving to "smite" my enemies and return me as the victor, or at the very least move to quickly open another door?

A Catholic Distance University online seminar on suffering I took at this time reminded me that "the teacher is always quiet during the test." I then remembered the Gulf War decades before and that God was hearing our prayers.

God has a plan.

Our present suffering, our present pain, was strengthening our family. Friends, former employees, and supportive board members and their families checked on us regularly. Our faith grew, and Patty and I began to pray together every morning, not just for ourselves, but for our families and for those hurting as we were. We also prayed for the healing and forgiveness of those who had hurt us so deeply.

The healing power of prayer is truly amazing. Our prayers began to focus less on ourselves and more on the needs of others. We thanked God for his love and for our marriage. We thanked God for our many blessings and for our friends and family. Our prayers brought us closer to God and closer to each other.

We began regular discussions about how God was moving to create something beautiful, something better, out of this hardship. Sometimes we simply borrowed a little faith and hope from one another to get through another day.

We prayed for healing and discovered that there was a whole army of friends and former co-workers who were lifting us up in prayer and healing our wounds. These prayer warriors were bringing us love and joy in the midst of our suffering.

We prayed for forgiveness for the vengeance we sought, and we found peace. In our fallen weakness, we discussed several heinous things we could do to "get even" for the cold-hearted injustice done to our family. Then we were reminded of the injustice done to our Lord on the cross, and we thanked God for another day of his grace.

We asked God why he allowed this to happen and we were reminded that one of the greatest gifts of creation is free will. We were reminded that God has blessed all mankind with it and for him to have interceded to protect us would have been to deny someone of that gift. Each person must choose how they will use this gift and each person will be held accountable for that choice. Some will use their free will for good, but some will not.

We remembered the stories of our sons. They told us about the injustices of the warlords and terrorist groups in Africa and about how innocent people were being stoned, starved, and brutalized. We remembered the suffering of the Iraqi people under Saddam and of the Christian martyrs in Mexico and the Middle East.

Suddenly our "suffering" became very trivial.

We knew that we had to trust and have the faith that God would take this hurtful event and turn it into something better. God would create. We have learned that God loves to create beauty.

We had a new plan. I would not return to the non-profit industry that I had worked in for twenty-five years. I would branch out and start over in a new industry where we could stay in the Piney Woods region of Texas, close to our family and friends. We would have to scale back a little, but we could make it.

We had a plan.

Months went by without a single job offer. Tensions were getting high and money was getting low. My job search radius began to grow larger and larger. Our prayer was that the Lord would open the one door that would allow us to continue to grow closer to one another and to God. The door where we would be able to continue in ministry and, above all, glorify God.

Months passed and we became desperate. In that desperation, we began to look farther and farther from home. I applied for jobs in areas that we never would have considered before. Our sons were in college 150 miles away and we couldn't bear the thought of moving far away from them. But suddenly, in our desperation, moving away from our family and friends, away from the house we built and the farm we loved became an option.

Little did we realize that what we were doing was giving God space to create in our lives. We realized that we had been putting God in a very small box. We were exerting our free will in a way that was limiting God's impact in our lives. We remembered: God loves to create.

We also realized another amazing truth: God will *always* work for the good of his children and his Church. God will take the greatest injustice and create something beautiful, *if we let him.*

Just as our savings were reaching the end and fear was beginning to creep back into our minds, an opportunity arose. God created, and God moved. Another non-profit reached out and offered me a better job than the one I had lost. We moved to a small, mid-western town in a state we had never even considered.

God took this horrible, faith-shaking event in our lives and transformed it into a moment of hope, peace, and grace. A new ministry and a new blessing await us here. It will be exciting to discover what the Lord has planned for us.

We came through another great, dark valley with God's help. It was one that we never thought we would find ourselves walking. It was a valley where we cried and faced hurt and depression. Some days we felt cold and alone, but some days we could see the Son and feel his warmth. Some days were better than others, but many days were dark and felt hopeless. It was a test and, as always, the teacher was silent.

What would our reaction be? Anger and moving away from God or prayerful hope and reaching out to him?

This world continues to be a place of great joy and a place of great pain. Such is the nature of our fallen world. Our task is to remain focused on God and on doing his will as the storm of life rages around us.

Our challenge is to recognize that sometimes people intentionally or unintentionally use God's gifts in ways that hurt others. But our great joy is to recognize that everything God created is good and that God is loving and faithful.

A former instructor of mine used to tell his seminary students, "If you're going to follow Jesus, sometimes you have to look good on wood." Sometimes bad things happen to good people. The way may be confusing, the path may be dark, but God is faithful, and he loves to create. Give God the chance and he will bring good out of suffering and move you into his new creation.

It is an awesome and a humbling thing to realize that the Creator of the Universe, the Alpha and the Omega, the Lord and Savior of all humankind knows each of us by name. He is the good Father, and he loves us and wants us to prosper, not as the world prospers, but to grow in love and hope and kindness. These are the things that bring us closer to God and to his salvation, to a new creation that he desires for us.

Postscript: Richard McLeon and his wife are in the process of being received into full communion with the Catholic Church, which is planned for Easter Vigil 2021 in the Catholic Diocese of Dodge City, Kansas.

Chapter 7

EPIPHANY IN JAIL

This is the story of how Aneel Aranha found his way to serving Christ after much personal struggle and suffering.

I was just thirteen or fourteen when I stopped believing in God. The reasons are numerous, but they aren't particularly relevant to this testimony. What is relevant is that my disbelief in God was total. He did not exist. Period.

As the years went by, I saw no reason to change my mind; if anything, I just grew increasingly certain that God was nothing more than an invention by people to explain the things they couldn't explain. The philosophers that I read only further reinforced my belief. And if intellectual certainty wasn't enough, my life itself seemed to bear witness to the nonexistence of God.

Arrogant and Proud

If you had met me when I was younger, you would have seen a man who had just about everything a man could possibly want. I had a beautiful wife and two lovely children. I ran a successful business with offices in three countries. I had all the things that the world would say were the signs of success.

But more than this, I was a man to whom nothing bad ever seemed to happen. I got into fights, accidents, and other situations that should have seen me arrested, injured, or even dead. But I walked out of each and every one of them without anything to show for them other than an increasing feeling of invincibility. I believed I was untouchable. I thought I could do anything I wanted.

And for a long time, I could.

In Free Fall

Then one day, things started changing. I sold my business to an American dot com company, but rather than cash out completely, I clung on to the major part thinking that I would make a lot more money in a couple of years. Hardly did I sell it and the dot com market crashed, and along with other companies, my own company went hurtling downward. I shrugged it off, believing as I always did that nothing bad could stick to me.

Sure enough, while the company continued to plunge, I got a job offer with a publishing company to edit one of their business titles and the title of vice president thrown in for good measure. And everything would have been great, except that less than three months later, the company began going down the tubes. I couldn't believe it. People started quitting, but I hung on, sure that things would get better—after all, I was untouchable, wasn't I?

The company went bust.

I kept waiting for the old "magic" to work, but it seemed to have gone. Where once everything I touched turned to gold, it seemed like everything I touched now turned to dust. And I began to get angry with the world as if it was the world's fault that things had started going bad for me.

Rage

One night in July, as my life continued to collapse with great rapidity around me, I went out drinking with some friends of mine. I wasn't an alcoholic but I was a rather heavy drinker, and like most drinkers, I thought that I had control over alcohol. I was to find out just how little control I had that night.

I don't remember returning home. I don't remember anything that followed other than a few hazy images until sometime in the morning, I found my bedroom filling with policemen and I knew I had done something terrible. Within fifteen minutes, I was in the police station. Five hours later, I was behind bars, locked up with rapists and drug pushers and murderers like an ordinary criminal.

I found out a little later what I had done. I had torn up my house, smashing some of those very symbols of prosperity I had been so proud off. I had hurt my wife so badly she had to be taken to the hospital. And I had pulled a knife on her threatening to kill her and my little daughter, who was then only six years old. I was not a very good husband or a very good father, but in a strange way, I loved my family, and it seemed crazy that I would do something like that to them, but in one of those rare moments of honesty that we are sometimes blessed with, I realized that in a rage—especially a drunken rage—I could have killed them all. The thought was horrific.

When I spoke to my wife later, I told her that I was sorry, but she wasn't interested in accepting my apology. She said she was going to take the children and leave me. And I knew she meant it because I could hear the fear in her voice and knew she was scared witless of me.

And I knew my life was over. In less than twelve months, I had lost everything I had, and when you don't have anything, then what is the point of living? I knew that when they let me out of jail, I would go for a swim one day on the beach and keep swimming. It was all over for me.

Jesus, Do You Exist?

I sat down in the corridor (all the cells were full) and wondered what happened to this man who thought he was invincible and how things had reached this point where death became the most appealing of options. As I brooded, I happened to notice a young man in the cell facing me. He was reading a Bible and there was a look of such peace on his face that he looked almost beatific. I found myself envying him, and even more so a moment later when I realized I had never known peace, not one day's peace in the twenty-five years gone by.

How did this guy manage it? Especially in a place like this which was sheer bedlam. There were three radios blasting three different kinds of music. There were people yelling and fighting with one another. There were people stomping up and down the cell block. But none of it seemed to bother this guy. I went up to him and asked him how he managed it. Looking up from the Bible he was reading, he smiled and said, "Jesus."

At any other time, I probably would have been scornful, but then, I was just conscious of this tremendous feeling of sadness. "Jesus," I thought. "Do you even exist? To be able to give people anything, much less peace?" I didn't believe it any more than I had a day earlier, but hope springs eternal in the human soul and death was too final a solution not to turn to one final possibility of saving myself. And I did.

"Jesus," I whispered. "If you're real, help me get out of this mess." I almost imagined I heard someone sigh.

The next time I spoke to my wife, I told her that I would do whatever it took to keep the family intact (I needed some anchor), and that included getting back to God. She didn't quite believe me, which was not surprising given my previous antipathy toward religion. I had been so sure that God didn't exist that I didn't let our two kids be baptized, my wife pray in the house, or permit her to bring anything of a religious nature into the home. However, she seemed prepared to give me a chance, and I was grateful because I meant what I said, and the very first morning after I was released, I went to church.

July 14, 2002

It was the first time in twenty-five years that I was walking voluntarily into a church—if you excluded my wedding ceremony, which to me was an exercise in role-playing. I participated in the Mass the best I could, which wasn't much really. I stood when everybody stood and sat when everybody sat, but I just couldn't bring myself to kneel. I was still too proud, too arrogant.

When the service was over, I went to meet the parish priest, Fr. John, who had celebrated Mass. I told him that I wanted to get back to God. He gave me a long-studied look before saying he wasn't sure of my sincerity and that I should go back to church and meditate for a while.

I stared at him in complete disbelief. Wasn't the fact that I was there an indication of my sincerity? But I was tired and wasn't inclined to argue—besides, there seemed to be an element of truth to what he said—so I returned to the church and sat down, not quite sure what I was supposed to do. My heart wanted to accept Jesus, my heart needed to accept Jesus, but my mind rebelled. I hadn't believed in God for twenty-five years! I had been so sure that God didn't exist that I hadn't even let my two kids—one fourteen, the other six—be baptized. How was I supposed to suddenly start believing he existed? I wanted to, but it was so difficult.

I looked around the church helplessly glancing at the various images hung on the walls, wondering what I should do, when I found my eyes drawn to a gold and black mosaic of Our Lady in one corner. It was a beautiful picture and I was admiring it, thinking how lovely the lady in it looked, when suddenly I heard her say, "Aneel, come to me."

I looked away, thinking my imagination was running wild, but then a moment later, I heard the voice again. This time there was no denying that I had actually heard it. It was so clear, I can still hear it in my head. "Aneel, come to me," she said. For a man who had lived his life on the altar of reason, this belonged to the story book world of fantasy, but to deny I heard that voice was tantamount to denying my very existence—or my sanity. I began to get scared.

"Aneel, don't be afraid. Come to me," the voice said for a third time.

It is perhaps fortuitous that there were only five or six people in the church at the time, otherwise I might never have done what I did. I got up and walked across the sanctuary to that mosaic. I found myself unable to look up at it for a long moment, but when I finally raised my eyes, I suddenly felt a wave of fire run through me filling every pore of my body, only the fire wasn't hot, it was cold, and was the most delicious sensation imaginable. It went on and on for nearly half a minute and was the most beautiful thing I had ever experienced.

And then I believed!

It is said that all you need to do is take one step towards God and he will cross miles and miles to get to you, and I saw evidence of this in the church that day. I was a man who wanted to get back home but was unable to find his way back. God didn't wait for me to ask for directions; he came and took me home. And even as God did that, he gave me the gift of faith. That was the first miracle.

I stayed on for the next Mass, and this time, when people knelt, I knelt too. It felt like the most natural thing in the world. I went for Communion and received Jesus in me for the first time in twenty-five years. And I experienced a feeling of peace in my heart like I had never experienced before. It was like I was one with the world, one with the universe, one with God. The sensation was utterly amazing.

I went back to the priest after the Mass, and this time, there weren't any questions about my sincerity. Very graciously, he took me under his wing, and over the course of a week, he gave me instruction on various aspects of Catholicism before he finally said I was ready to make my confession.

The Love of Jesus

I wanted to make a good confession, so that night, I sat down in front of the computer and started typing out my sins. They went on, and on, and on. I discovered I had committed every sin imaginable, short of murder, though I was perhaps guilty of that too. When you think something in your head and want it with your heart, the deed is as good as done, and I had committed murder in heart and mind.

I was horrified! Not so much by the sheer volume of my sins but by the fact that I hadn't even realized that I had been doing anything wrong. The next day, I went to

Fr. John and made my confession. At the end of it, he told me to say a Rosary as penance. I was shocked. A Rosary! Just a Rosary! For twenty-five years of sinning!

"That's not enough," I said.

"What do you suggest?" he asked mildly.

"I don't know. Make it twenty-five Rosaries; one for each year I've been away from God."

The priest said okay, but I couldn't help feeling I was still getting off light. This wasn't justice in my world. I wanted to be lashed, scourged, made to carry a cross, even be crucified.

Fr. John was a wise man, and he seemed to discern what I was thinking.

"Aneel," he said. "I want you to know something. This is not punishment. Your sins have been forgiven. All of them. Jesus paid the price for them when he died on the cross."

It was at that moment that the full love of Jesus struck me and I swore to myself that I would try to never, ever do anything in my life to hurt this wonderful man again.

Further Transformation

I returned home and began dismantling my old life, systematically burning, smashing, and otherwise voiding myself of anything that I felt would be an offense to Jesus. Bootleg CD's and video cassettes, pirated software, and a collection of pornography that was as vast as it was depraved were all destroyed along with letters and photographs from my old girlfriends.

As if in appreciation of my efforts to purify myself, Jesus himself stepped in and performed a second miracle in my life. He totally wiped away my desire for alcohol. A single drink at that stage might have blown my new life to bits, but now there was not the slightest temptation to imbibe, not even when I was in a room full of people who were drinking.

But not all was smooth sailing. I would sometimes still fly into wild rages. I always had a bad temper, manic even, but it usually took some extreme provocation to arouse it. Now I lost it for the slightest reason. The smallest thing was enough to set me off. My anger never lasted for more than a few seconds, but I could wreck havoc during that time.

I did everything I could think of to curb these explosive outbursts, but it seemed like the more I tried, the less I succeeded. On one occasion when I felt my anger rise, I dropped to my knees and said all three mysteries of the Rosary back-to-back. The instant I got to my feet, the anger burst out of me like a starved animal set free from its cage, explosive and wild.

For someone who was trying so hard to make up to God for all that he had been up to, this was a nightmare, and the only penance I could think of doing was fasting. I hoped that this would not only get God to forgive me but also make him give me strength to control my temper, but this didn't seem to work. On the contrary, on one occasion, after I had fasted for three days consuming nothing but water, I lost my temper more heavily than I ever had before.

Utterly frustrated, I begged Jesus. "Why are you letting this happen? You can see how hard I am trying! Can't you please help me?"

That night as I lay in bed, I suddenly felt my head get heavy as a rock. Everything went dark and I felt something like a hand reach out and grip my brain. My first thought was it was the devil and he was out to get me for tossing him so unceremoniously out of my life and I freaked. But a voice I thought I recognized as Jesus's told me not to worry. That was easier said than done—this was my brain! I told my wife to get a rosary and a crucifix, and clutching one in each hand, I told Jesus that if it indeed was him, to go ahead and do whatever he wanted. Agonizing pain followed, but despite it, I dropped off to sleep at some point.

When I woke up the next morning, I didn't feel any different and shrugged off the entire experience as the result of an increasingly overactive imagination. But a week later, I didn't react at all when something occurred that normally would have made me blow my fuse. Then, I realized that I had not lost my temper once since that night!

Two Months Later

Two months later, my wife and I went for a five-day live-in retreat in southern India. I had heard that this retreat center was supposed to have brought about amazing transformations in the lives of those who attended. I figured I already was transformed, but if there were to be further improvements in my life, I would only be too happy.

When we reached the retreat center, I saw a large sign at the gate that said smoking was strictly prohibited inside the premises. I grimaced. I still retained much of my contempt for rules—arrogance dies hard—and I had no intention of following this one. Besides, I wasn't sure I could follow it even if I wanted to. I was a chain smoker and I used to smoke three packets of cigarettes a day, five in the days when I drank. That is sixty to a hundred cigarettes a day!

I had heard that people who attended the retreat quit smoking, and if that happened in my case, I would be delighted, but I wasn't taking any chances: I had four cartons of Benson & Hedges in my backpack!

We checked in and then went for the first session. After it was over, I rushed up to my room, and in the twenty minute break we had been given, I smoked five cigarettes one after another. If I ever needed evidence as to how hopelessly addicted to tobacco I was, this was it.

During the next session, one of the speakers spoke about the sanctity of life and how it was an unforgivable sin to take life, even if it was one's own. The statement was made almost in passing, but the effect it had on me was enormous. I wanted to quit smoking right then and there, but quite honestly didn't know how to. I had been a smoker since my early teens and had never quit for more than a couple of days at a time despite trying my best several times.

We broke off for lunch, which turned out to be entirely vegetarian. I loathed vegetables, and unless they formed part of a meat dish, I avoided them altogether. "I'm a pure non-vegetarian," I liked to say. Deciding not to make a big deal of it, however, I served myself a small portion, glad that it didn't take much of an effort to put everything away.

I returned straight to the retreat hall after lunch. My thoughts were still very much occupied with how to give up smoking when I felt Jesus say, "Aneel, give it up."

"I don't know how," I replied.

"Just quit," he said. "Leave the rest to me."

That evening, there was a session called "Surrender" where you surrendered something to the Lord. This could be a weakness that you had, or a burden that weighed you down, or—as in my case—a habit you couldn't give up.

This seemed to be my cue. I got up, went to my room, and after collecting all the cigarettes I had, I returned and dumped everything into a trash bin that was placed in the session room for this very purpose.

And my addiction was gone! There were no withdrawal symptoms. There was no unbearable craving for a cigarette. There was no moodiness or grumpiness. And a habit I had thought I could never break was broken with only the effort it took to make a decision, a decision to surrender it to the Lord.

The Anointing

The following morning, we were in the middle of prayer when I suddenly felt a massive wave of electricity shoot through my body. It is an experience that goes beyond words, and the closest I can come to describing it is by comparing it to electrocution. It was like I was plugged into an electric machine and someone had turned the juice on. I had no clear idea what was happening, except I knew that something momentous was taking place. When it ended, I felt more alive than I had ever felt in my life. But at the same time, strangely empty, as if I had been given a taste of paradise only to have it taken away.

I waited for the experience to recur, wanting it, needing it, but the day passed into night without anything happening other than a few shivers that might have been from a breeze that had begun blowing from seemingly nowhere. Just before the session ended, I engaged Jesus in some intense conversation, mostly impassioned appeals for him to repeat the experience. I promised him a total surrender of self in return; I promised him I would never sin again if I could help it; I promised him that I'd do anything and everything he wanted me to do, even die for him.

"Are you sure?" I felt Jesus ask, before adding softly, "You might have to."

"Yes, Lord," I said with utter and complete conviction.

And then I got blasted again, this time nearly off my feet. For about five minutes—it could easily have been ten or twenty—I had this current pouring through me, unceasingly. The experience I had in the morning was wonderful, but it was nothing like this. This was raw, naked power that I knew was from God himself. This was the power that parted the Red Sea. This was the power that smashed the walls of Jericho. This was the power that helped Samson bring down the temple. This was the power of God himself.

And I knew that my life would never ever be the same again. And it hasn't been.

Postscript: In January 2004, Aneel founded the Holy Spirit Interactive (HSI) Catholic lay apostolate, which is dedicated to strengthening the faith of Christians and spreading the Gospel around the world. Through its various ministries and activities, which include Schools of Discipleship, retreats, seminars, publishing, radio, film, TV, and a popular website, HSI reaches several million people each year. For more, see www.hsiweb.org.

Chapter 8

IS MY SON DEAD?

This is the testimony of Terri Thomas in dealing with the sudden and unexpected death of her young adult son.

If someone told you one of your worst nightmares would become a reality, what would you do? This happened to me on October 15, 2015, the day I entered into the most difficult period of my life.

It was about 11:00 a.m. when a coworker interrupted a women's Bible study I was in and asked me to gather my things and come with her. I could see it was serious, so I asked her what was going on. She said that my husband had called and asked her to take me home. I blindly followed her, and as soon as I was in her car, I called Dan and asked him what was happening. My mind was anxiously racing to thoughts my daughters, Nicole and Erin, thinking that something had happened to one of them. It didn't even cross my mind that anything could be wrong with my twenty-six-year-old son, Brett, because he was sleeping when I left our house that morning. He was in between projects for his job and was home for two weeks, relaxing. Dan proceeded to tell me that the paramedics were at our house and that Brett was unresponsive. I was shocked! I could not process what he was saying, but I desperately hoped that Brett was somehow still alive.

I arrived home and found several police cars and an ambulance in the driveway. I ran inside and was immediately greeted by a police officer in the foyer. I found Dan and a detective in the kitchen. My hopes vanished as soon as I looked at their faces. I asked if Brett was dead, and they very solemnly told me that he was. I felt as if my heart shattered into a million pieces, yet at the same time, it was as if I was inquiring about someone else's son. It was completely surreal. I asked if I could see him, but my request was denied because his room was considered a potential crime scene until they could determine the cause of death.

Shortly after that, my pastor and a deacon from our church arrived. I remember asking Fr. John questions like, "Why didn't God warn me about this?" and "What have I done wrong?" He didn't have the answers but just listened compassionately. Before they left, I asked that they let people know that we needed time alone to begin to process this trauma. Two of my best friends showed up anyway, but I was very thankful they did. Dan was busy with the police, detectives, and coroner, so it was a great consolation to have them there.

Eventually, I was allowed to see my son's precious body. I remember looking at him and rubbing his face and his hair. He was so handsome! It was shocking to see and touch his lifeless body. Even at this moment, it didn't feel like it was really happening. I don't know how long I stood there in the foyer looking at him, but I remember I was outside when they wheeled his body out, placed it in the hearse, and drove away—something I couldn't process then, but later, thought about a lot.

As for the cause of his death, all they could surmise was that it wasn't suicide or an overdose, so there would have to be an autopsy, and that wouldn't happen until the following week. The unknown cause of death was extremely difficult to deal with and added an extra layer of suffering to our confusion and broken hearts.

One thing I remember doing right away was praying the Fatima Sacrifice Prayer repeatedly: "Oh Jesus, I offer this for love of you, in reparation for the outrages against the Immaculate Heart of Mary and the conversion of poor sinners." That prayer had become a part of my everyday life over the past twenty-two years and had enabled me to find peace in many difficult situations, and now I needed it more than ever!

After everyone left, things happened so fast. We had to shatter our daughters' hearts and tell them the terrible news. Nicole (24), was living in Charleston, South Carolina, and Erin (22), was attending college in Milledgeville, Georgia. They were both completely devastated. We made arrangements for Nicole to fly home that evening, and then we left to bring Erin home from college.

We made many other phone calls throughout the day. Every person was stunned. It was extremely difficult to keep saying the words, "Brett is dead."

That night, the four of us slept in our bedroom, and all through the night, I could hear sobbing. It was terrible. The world felt dark and gloomy. The future seemed empty and unbearable. I kept thinking, "How am I going to make it for the rest of my life without Brett? How are we going to do this?" For each of us, our own suffering was greatly compounded by knowing how much the other three were suffering.

We had to wait for almost a week to find out from the coroner that a cause for Brett's death could not be determined from the autopsy, so the next step would be toxicology testing, and it could take up to four months for the results! It was so difficult to wait that long to officially learn what on earth could have happened. This added yet another layer of suffering that I offered up to God as a sacrifice.

I could not sit idle, however, and wait on the results, so I began my own investigation. God seemed to be meeting me in my efforts by providing passwords to Brett's social media accounts and friends of his that came forward to honestly answer my many questions. Unfortunately, it was one heartbreak after another. The pain was so great that, at times, I felt such utter anguish that I didn't know how I would survive. Like so many other suffering people, I could say like Job: "O that my vexation were weighed, and all my calamity laid in the balances! For then it would be heavier than the sand of the sea" (Job 6:2–3).

We discovered that on the night of October 14, he had taken what he thought was prescription pain medication. The speculation was that it was "dirty" because what he consumed wasn't enough to hurt him. When the toxicology results came back, we learned that it had been laced with fentanyl. It was more than he could handle and it killed him. This was devastating.

In addition to an overwhelming sense of guilt, I also experienced mortal anguish, sadness, confusion, and anger—sometimes directed at Brett, sometimes at myself, and sometimes at God. The emotions directed at God comprise the arena where the greatest struggle took place. One of the things that I wrestled with during the first few months is why God would have allowed me to be completely in the dark about this. I felt that he had not only abandoned me but even went so far as to allow me to be deceived into believing that Brett was okay the night before.

I say this because I wasn't an absentee parent or fair-weather Catholic. For the previous twenty-two years, I had been trying to live as a true Christian. I was actively involved in my children's lives and prayed continually for guidance in order to raise them to be good Catholics. I attempted to discern and follow God's will in all areas of my life—nothing was off limits—and I was diligent in my efforts to improve, what was for many years, a troubled marriage for the sake of my family.

Brett's death was a complete blindside! None of us saw this coming. It was so hard to process in light of this closeness with God that I felt and all the answered prayers that I had experienced. But in spite of this confusion and suffering, the virtues of faith, hope, and charity were and continue to be the means that Christ has used to carry me through this period of intense darkness; without them, I would have despaired.

Foundation of Faith

In order to understand why I feel this way, I'll share some of my background. I am a cradle Catholic. My father is an ordained permanent deacon, and throughout my life, both of my parents were active in the Catholic Charismatic Renewal. Growing up, I saw my parents live a joy-filled life in the midst of intense suffering by following God's will as manifested through the teachings of the Catholic Church. As a result of their "obedience of faith" (Rom 16:26) and constant recourse to prayer, I witnessed God clearly leading them and helping them. As a young child, this made a big impression on me.

I witnessed my mother practice heroic virtue. She was pregnant eight times, but only three of us survived. She has the Rh factor, and in spite of all the confusion following the Second Vatican Council, she remained faithful to the Church's teaching as articulated in *Humanae Vitae*. What made her obedience extra difficult were the priests who encouraged her to use the birth control pill. Her OBGYN did the same thing, especially after her fifth pregnancy, because every time another child was conceived, it put her life at risk. At the end of her eighth pregnancy and the loss of her fifth baby, my parents were introduced to Natural Family Planning, which they successfully practiced for the rest of their fertile years.

I also witnessed my parents suffer greatly through the severe test of my brother's mental illness. When he was twenty-one years old, he suffered through a psychotic episode that changed his life forever. My sister and I agonized over his mental deterioration, but my parents were always there for us and their strong faith was a wonderful example. Around this time, my mother read Pope St. John Paul II's encyclical *On the Christian Meaning of Human Suffering* (*Salvifici Doloris*) which helped her find peace. She did her best to explain it to us, and although I couldn't quite grasp the concept, it was a seed planted in my heart that would bear fruit in the future.

Conversion Through Surrender

In spite of my parents' wonderful example of faith, however, as I grew older, I strayed from God. I, like Adam and Eve, wanted the forbidden fruit. I didn't think I could be happy following God's will.

I had a great time for a while, but eventually wore myself out from focusing too much on my social life. I ended up dropping out of college twenty hours short of graduating. After returning home, I went to work at a finance company where I met Dan.

Our relationship started off on shaky ground, however, as I was four months pregnant on our wedding day. After Brett was born, I stayed home with him and took on babysitting jobs. Nicole was born seventeen months later, and Erin three years after that. But throughout these early years, Dan wasn't ready to settle down. He was gone a lot, either traveling or going out after work. Women were always flirting with him and he didn't do anything to discourage that. Speaking of myself, I was insecure, controlling, and overly sensitive, so needless to say, without mentioning any more of his faults, we had issues.

After eight years of blaming Dan for everything and trying to solve our marriage problems without God's help, I was exhausted and we were on the brink of divorce. It seemed logical to me that God would agree that divorce was best, but with three children to care for, the prospect of being a single mother terrified me. So one evening when I had reached my limit, I went to my bedroom and cried. At that moment, my parents' wonderful example paid off and I surrendered my life to God, telling him that I was worn out from doing things my way and was ready to do his will 100 percent; I just begged him to make it clear to me. The last thing I said as I fell asleep was, "If you can save my marriage, please do so."

Pope St. John Paul II taught, "The springs of divine power gush forth through human weakness" (*Salvifici Doloris*, VI, 27). That's the best way to describe what happened next. That moment of complete surrender gave God the opening to come into my life in a powerful way, and I began to see his loving care manifesting itself in ways I could clearly recognize—just like I had witnessed him do for my parents. This brought me so much joy!

One of the most powerful ways that God came into my life during this time was through our Blessed Mother. I began to pray the Rosary each day, and from there, she led me into a relationship with Jesus in the sacraments. I hadn't been to the sacrament of Reconciliation for many years, so I asked her to help me make a good confession. As I was praying the Rosary, she gave me a wonderful grace—she brought to mind the serious sins that I had committed since my last confession, along with a deep understanding of why they were wrong and a sincere sorrow for them. I vividly remember that there was a vigil Mass going on when I came out of the confessional and feeling a strong desire (from the inside of me) to attend. Prior to this, I attended out of obligation only, and even then, not regularly. It was at this point that Our Lady led me into a deeper relationship with Jesus in the Eucharist.

Consequently, my moral life took on new energy as I tried to please God with every thought, word, and action, especially in my roles as a wife and a mother. I am glad to say that this past December, we celebrated our thirtieth wedding anniversary. Our marriage didn't turn around overnight. It's been a long, hard journey, but it has gotten easier over the years, especially the last ten. There is absolutely no way we would be married today without the grace of God that comes to us through the Church. As baptized Catholics, God has literally opened to us the treasures of his house.

Recourse to Mary, Our Blessed Mother

Living in relationship with our Blessed Mother, I trusted in her intercession for my family and friends.

Dan grew up as a Baptist but didn't retain much of those beliefs, except that he was pretty sure Catholics shouldn't have any kind of devotion to Our Blessed Mother. This was an obstacle to him becoming Catholic. I, on the other hand, was growing in love for the Catholic faith, and Our Blessed Mother was a big part of that. I wanted to share this with my family, so I asked God to help him with this.

About this time, we learned that a former coworker's nine-year-old son had been diagnosed with a brain tumor. I was devastated for them! A priest had told me that every time we combine offering sacrifices with praying the Rosary, God sends angels. I immediately began praying a decade of the Rosary each day with my children for "the boy with the brain tumor." I also taught them to offer small sacrifices for him (e.g., eating the vegetable they didn't like, picking up toys without being asked, etc.). It was not easy to do this. Many days, the Rosary decade was poorly prayed, and some days we missed it altogether, but I persevered. My concern for their family kept me going. As we prayed and offered these small sacrifices, I frequently reminded my children that God was sending angels to help him. Often times, Dan would smirk as I said this.

About a year later, Dan was going to a business convention. I tried to stop him from going because of the immoral behavior so prevalent there, but he went anyway. Praise God! While there, he ran into the boy's father. They spent the entire day together. He told Dan about some of the miracles that had taken place in the past year. He said that when his son was on a ventilator, he began to suffer from depression and they were very worried about him. One day, out of the blue, his spirits lifted. At different times he would excitedly point to the space next to the doctor or between his parents. When he could talk again, he would say, "Dad, there is an angel next to you!" or "There is an angel next to Mom!" He told them the angels were there to help him. One day, several months later, he was crying, and when his parents asked him why he was upset, he told them he wouldn't be seeing the angels anymore because he no longer needed them.

Dan came home and told me this. I couldn't believe it! God really had sent angels. A few months later, Dan entered the RCIA program and he was baptized the following Easter.

God's Natural and Supernatural Gifts

As I stated before, my son's death was a complete blindside; in no way did we see it coming. Initially, I was utterly confused and in the deepest darkness. It felt like God was mocking me; that in all these years I must have been presumptuous about my relationship with him and was instead far-removed from his grace. I scrutinized as many of my past actions as I could recall and went to the sacrament of Reconciliation numerous times for absolution and to alleviate the guilt I felt. It made me question everything, especially myself. I questioned all my answered prayers and my parents' prayers before that, and all the conclusions I drew because of them.

I am still in a place of darkness, not because I don't trust God, but because his ways truly are so hard to understand at times. The only response is to believe without understanding at all and to pray, "Jesus, I trust in you."

On October 15, I woke up at 6:00 a.m., and in my prayer time, I meditated on Isaiah 55:8–9: "For my thoughts are not your thoughts, neither are your ways my ways, said the LORD. For as the heavens are higher than the earth, so are my ways higher than your ways, and my thoughts than your thoughts."

I didn't know at the time, but right upstairs, Brett had already died.

Here is what I do know. Revelation 7:17 states, "For the Lamb in the midst of the throne will be their shepherd, and he will guide them to springs of living water; and God will wipe away every tear from their eyes." This is absolutely true!

As I grow in my Catholic faith, I have learned to rely on the gifts God has provided, springs of life-giving water, to help me as I navigate the journey through grief and suffering. He gently calls us all through the circumstances and difficulties in our lives to make good and proper use of them.

Some of these gifts occur naturally and some of them are given to us supernaturally. I do believe that the supernatural gifts are the most important because they enable the natural gifts to work more effectively. The natural gifts alone would not have been sufficient to provide the healing and peace that I needed.

I do want to say that many people experience a misplaced sense of guilt if they experience any type of relief from sadness or any joy at all, as if the deceased person would be upset with this. I believe this is a temptation we must fight. I don't believe Brett thinks I must not love him very much if I'm not sad all the time, as if the measure of my continual sadness equals the measure of my love for him. I do believe that any relief and joy that I experience is because he is praying to God for this, and

I am honoring his prayers if I open myself up to God's help.

The following are examples of the *natural* gifts that helped my family during our time of need.

The Support of Family and Friends

I am so grateful for the love and support that we received in our darkest hour. These people carried us when we couldn't carry ourselves. Each act of kindness touched our hearts deeply and lifted our spirits. I asked that, in lieu of flowers, others have a Mass offered for the repose of Brett's soul. There were over four hundred Masses offered for him. One person even set up a Gregorian Mass series to begin on November 2, All Souls Day. All of this was a wonderful consolation to us!

I am also grateful I had particular people to whom I was able to vent. It's too much to expect immediate family members to be able to handle that. Dan, Nicole, and Erin were suffering so much themselves that I couldn't expect them to deal with my emotions as well, so I turned to my parents. I would call them to cry or to express the anger I was feeling towards God, Brett, or myself. They would just listen without trying to fix anything. They would cry with me when I was upset or be joyful with me when I shared a consolation that God had given me. This was so helpful to me in the healing process.

Pets, Babies, Exercise, and Tears

I believe each one of these are natural anti-depressants. Every time I look at my dog with love, it lifts my spirits. Just in their presence alone, pets of all kinds can provide a lot of comfort.

Even more so, babies cultivate a warmth in our hearts, and we can't help but smile when we look at them, especially when I look at my new grandson (born on Brett's birthday in May, 2019).

God designed our bodies to need exercise, and through the release of endorphins when we exercise, our anxieties decrease and our energy levels increase, often creating an improved outlook on life. I have felt the benefits of exercise, so I know it enhances my well-being.

Finally, studies have shown that emotional tears are good for us. They contain stress hormones that are expelled from the body through crying, unlike reflex tears that are 98 percent water. Crying also stimulates the production of endorphins. I know I always feel better after a good cry!

The Wisdom to Live in the Present Moment

My family and I had to live one day at a time, especially for the first two years. It was more than we could bear to think of never seeing Brett again in this life. Thinking of the future without him, even only as far into it as the next day, was excruciating. Every morning, I would wake up and pray, "With your help, Lord, I can make it through today without Brett." I learned that God's grace is always with us in the present moment. We don't have the grace and strength for the future yet, but we will when it gets here in real time. Living in anticipatory anxiety about the difficulty entailed in carrying a particular cross is a recipe for poor health—physically and psychologically. Now that it is almost four years later, I am able to think about the future without it causing me anxiety.

The Witness of Others

The witness of other Christians who have endured great suffering is very helpful, especially those who were transformed by their difficulties instead of getting stuck in them or transmitting their pain to others. Their stories are a source of encouragement and provide a great sense of hope that life, with God's grace, can be lived fruitfully and with purpose in spite of the difficulties and trials we encounter.

Advice from the Saints

The following are suggestions I found helpful from St. Thomas Aquinas about finding relief from sadness:

- Treat yourself to something small—a donut, cup of your favorite coffee, fresh flowers.
- Take a nap and a shower.
- Contemplate truth and beauty in a good book, nature, or music.

- Do something you enjoy—a hobby, gardening, dinner out with friends, etc.
- Look for ways to help others.

On the other hand, God's *supernatural* gifts come to us through the Church and elevate our suffering to a supernatural level. They give us the ability to find meaning in our suffering in a way that the natural gifts can't. While the natural gifts enable us to cope with our suffering, the supernatural gifts enable us to make a gift of ourselves in our suffering. Some of these gifts were already operating in my life before Brett died, but since his death, they are operating at a much deeper level.

The Eucharist

Shortly after I surrendered my life to God twenty-two years ago, I read a book that my parents had titled *Rosary Meditations from Mother Teresa of Calcutta: Loving Jesus with the Heart of Mary: Eucharistic Meditations on the Fifteen Mysteries of the Rosary.* This book describes how Jesus longs for us to come to Mass and spend time with him in Adoration, and unfortunately, in most churches, he is left alone in the tabernacle. As I read this book, my heart began to burn with the desire to console him. I rearranged my schedule so that I could attend daily Mass followed by a time of prayer before the tabernacle. During this time, I began to experience his love and closeness in a profound way, and my heart was literally set on fire with love for God!

To nurture my children's faith, twice a week I would take them to 7:00 a.m. Mass followed by breakfast on the way to school. They loved this, but it was a sacrifice because we had to get up earlier. One night, I was struggling with whether or not this was God's will. I was up late and remembered at 11:00 p.m. that I still had to make cupcakes. At the time, I was also participating in a Protestant Bible study on the Lord's Prayer. That day, I shared that "Give us this day our daily bread" for Catholics refers to the Eucharist. I had cited 1 Kings 19:7 as a prefigurement of the strength the Eucharist would provide for us in the long, hard journey to heaven: "And the angel of the Lord came again the second time, and touched him, and said to him: Arise, eat: for thou hast yet a great way to go'" (DV).

I felt interior turmoil about sharing that, and I was praying for God to let me know if it was okay. I finally went to bed about 1:00 a.m., and out of exhaustion and confusion, I decided not to set my alarm for 5:30 a.m. I prayed, "Dear Lord, if you want me to continue to take them to Mass like this, please wake me up."

At 5:30 a.m. sharp, I heard an audible voice say: "Arise, eat: for thou hast yet a great way to go." I believe it was my guardian angel! I joyfully and energetically jumped out of bed. I knew the Lord was telling me to keep making this sacrifice, and it gave me peace about sharing that in the Bible study.

Since Brett's death, I realize, now more than ever, that the strength for this long, hard journey comes from receiving our Savior in Holy Communion. Carrying this cross is hard. His strength begins where my natural ability ends, but much like an antibiotic or a vitamin, I cannot "feel" what he is doing to heal and strengthen me at the exact moment I consume him. As time goes on, however, the effect becomes more and more perceptible.

For example, after Brett died, I continued to attend daily Mass as often as possible, but I could not worship God spontaneously for several months. During this time, the liturgy of the Mass carried me, like a passenger on a train, to the throne of God to worship him. I would just listen and let the prayers of the Mass wash over me. Eventually, I was able to worship God again with my whole heart.

I also understand, more deeply now, that I don't go to Mass to be merely a passive recipient of God's grace but also to offer myself with Jesus to the Father for the salvation of the world. Because I am a member of his Mystical Body (the Church) and he lives in me (Gal 2:20), my offering has merit—eternal value. Receiving Jesus in Holy Communion strengthens me to make this offering of everything to him as a gift—my prayers, works, joys, sorrows, and sufferings. What a high calling we have as Christians!

Not only that, I believe that Brett is with me at Mass. I am worshiping God in communion with him because our Mass on earth is a participation in the heavenly liturgy.

Redemptive Suffering

"In my deepest wound I saw your glory, and it dazzled me" (St. Augustine). I learned about redemptive suffering for the first time in 1997 during prayer before our Lord in the tabernacle. Growing up, I was familiar with the phrase "Offer it up!" but I didn't understand what it meant. Unfortunately, I took it to mean "Just deal with it please!" Knowing the truth is life-changing!

The first eight years of my marriage were full of heartaches, but at the time, I didn't understand what to do with this pain. I knew that if I allowed myself to dwell on these feelings, I wouldn't be able to focus on caring for my children, so I repressed them.

One of the first things our Lord taught me was the eternal value of pain when it is offered as a sacrifice. As I sat before him in the Blessed Sacrament, one by one, he would gently bring to mind the painful memories I had repressed. I would feel the sadness and then offer that memory up for specific intentions.

For example, I learned to offer to God:

- any loneliness I experienced (for the intention that Jesus would never be left alone in the Blessed Sacrament),
- my faults and failures (for the intention that his divine love would triumph in every heart),
- all the misunderstandings in my life (for the intention that his love in the Eucharist would be understood by all),
- feelings of rejection (for the intention that his love in the Eucharist would be accepted by all),
- and feelings of not being appreciated (for

the intention that he would be appreciated by all).

At the time, our parish tabernacle was in a side chapel and very few people knew about it. Eucharistic Adoration took place on the first Friday of the month for a couple hours, and only a handful of people attended. I greatly longed for everyone to experience his love, so I continually offered all of my heartaches for our parish to have perpetual Eucharistic Adoration.

About a year later, I followed an inspiration from God and successfully initiated the efforts to begin perpetual Adoration. The joy I felt from seeing so many people deep in prayer before our Lord far outweighed any pain I had experienced in my marriage, and I began to understand the value of redemptive suffering. Those painful memories are now what I consider some of my greatest blessings. They no longer have the power to stir up any negative feelings because they have been completely transformed by God's love. Christ received the offering of my broken heart as a precious gift—he didn't belittle my feelings. He used them to draw me closer to him, and he valued the offering of my sufferings so much that he made each one into a channel of grace for others.

Around the same time, I encountered the story of Our Lady of Fatima, which touched my heart deeply and confirmed the value of redemptive suffering. Our Lady told the three children, who were seven, nine, and ten years old at the time, "Pray much and make sacrifices for sinners, for many souls go to hell because there is no one to pray and offer sacrifices for them." Earlier, Our Lady had asked them, "Are you willing to offer yourselves to God and bear all the sufferings He wills to send you as an act of reparation for the conversion of sinners?" They said they were. Our Lady replied, "Then you are going to have much to suffer, but the grace of God will be your comfort."

Mary then taught them a prayer to pray when making a sacrifice or patiently bearing a suffering or difficulty: "Oh Jesus, I offer this for love of you, in reparation for the outrages against the Immaculate Heart of Mary and the conversion of poor sinners." Right away, I began to offer my daily difficulties for this intention and have spent over two decades trying to live this way. Somehow, praying that prayer in the midst of suffering opens it up to the presence of the Risen Christ and transforms it into a prayer of intercession for others and keeps it from negatively affecting us.

God is using this habit of "offering up" my sufferings and difficulties as a prayer of intercession for others, as well as to help me today in my experience of grief. At times, the waves of grief wash over me like a tidal wave and it literally feels like I am drowning in the Dead Sea. Based on my past experiences, however, I believe that it is God's desire to transform these waves into living water. As I offer each one to God, Jesus takes it, unites it with his perfect sacrifice, and uses it as a channel of grace for others. The Church teaches that this will increase the flow of God's grace in the world. God allows us to see some of what he does with this offering, but most of it will be seen only in heaven.

I made a prayer list and as each wave of grief comes, I take it out and pray, "Lord, I offer my broken heart, my anguish to you for these intentions." I have offered up more waves of suffering in the last four years than in all the past twenty-two years combined. It doesn't take the pain away, but it does take the edge off it. I have hope that God will use them to bless others abundantly and that gives me joy and greatly helps in the healing process.

The Help of Our Blessed Mother

I include the Blessed Mother here also because I want to reiterate the special role she plays in my life. Her intercession has always brought me closer to God in ways that were instrumental and manageable for me in each circumstance. In the early days of my grieving, I would have flashbacks about all the events that happened the day of Brett's death. The traumatic events were all jumbled up in my head. I knew that I needed to grieve these memories and not ignore them. I asked our Blessed Mother to help me, and I believe that she led me to get a journal and write each memory down in the order of when it took place.

At different times, I would pick up my journal, read it, and cry, and then offer each memory to God as a sacrifice. Doing this has really helped me to connect with God and our Blessed Mother through my suffering, and this has enabled me to accept what happened and to find peace in a very difficult situation.

The Experience of Joy and Sorrow Simultaneously

To my surprise, I discovered that extreme sorrow and anguish can peacefully coexist with joy in my heart. Joy and sorrow are not incompatible. They are not opposed to each other. It is a profound mystery, but because of the presence of the Risen Christ in my soul and in my suffering, it is possible to experience both emotions at the same time. Before Brett died, this seemed impossible. I think about, miss, and feel sad about him continually, but I have peace and experience joy at the same time.

Scripture and the Teachings of the Catholic Faith

Closely connected to all of this are Scripture and the teachings of the Catholic faith about how suffering fits into God's plan for our lives. It is incredibly helpful to know that God is far more concerned with our eternal welfare than making us perfectly happy here and now. This earthly life is not paradise—it's a preparation for paradise in heaven. It's a time of testing, a time to grow and to allow God to increase our capacity to love him for all eternity. It is a time to live by the dark night of faith, which means believing in God's love even when he seems absent, distant, or asleep on the job, a time to grow in merit, and suffering is a big part of all of this.

As stated by St. Peter, "In this you rejoice, though now for a little while you may have to suffer various trials, so that the genuineness of your faith, more precious than gold which though perishable is tested by fire, may redound to praise and glory and honor at the revelation of Jesus Christ. Without having seen him you love him; though you do not now see him you believe in him and rejoice with unutterable and exalted joy. As the outcome of your faith you obtain the salvation of your souls" (1 Pt 1:6–9).

Our secular, hedonistic culture does not understand this and therefore does not understand the deeper purpose and meaning of suffering. How different is the way that Jesus taught us: "If any man would come after me, let him deny himself and take up his cross and follow me" (Mt 16:24).

Even though this sounds like a way deprived of fulfillment, it is the exact opposite. We are not meant to endure suffering as Christ did with our own strength, so the crosses that we carry become the very means to a deeper union with God who makes them bearable. This supernatural union with a loving Being, infinitely higher and greater than ourselves, is the conduit of true and lasting joy and "the peace of God, which passes all understanding," (Phil 4:7).

The death of my precious son is a cross that I will carry for the rest of my earthly life, and I know that God is with me, helping me to follow Christ in offering it as a sacrifice—a prayer of intercession for others. One morning, I was crying and offering my shattered heart to God. I was telling him that I wanted him to use it as a perpetual sacrifice for others, even if I didn't consciously tell him that at each moment. Immediately, God brought to my mind an image of the candles in church that burn continually. We light those candles for a prayer intention and the prayer remains before God even after we leave. I sensed that God was telling me that the offering of my shattered heart was like a candle burning perpetually before him. Even when I am occupied with the busyness of life and my mind isn't consciously thinking about it, my offering is still as effective as when I am.

My thoughts were then led to the red sanctuary lamp that unceasingly burns before the tabernacle as a better image of my offering as a living lamp burning with love before his Eucharistic Presence. This touched me deeply because I greatly desire that people understand and appreciate his love for us in the Eucharist.

God's Gift of Peace

In the months following Brett's death, I experienced different forms of anxiety: an oppressive, gloomy outlook for the future, a hyper-sense of concern for my family's safety, and a desperate need to know why God allowed it to happen. God gradually healed me of all three of these by replacing each one with a supernatural peace.

Anxiety About the Future

Sadness and feelings of depression are a normal part of grief, but I have learned that when there is an overwhelming sense of sadness, or feelings of gloom and doom continually present, there is something more going on—a supernatural evil presence: "For we are not contending against flesh and blood, but against the principalities, against the powers, against the world rulers of this present darkness, against the spiritual hosts of wickedness in the heavenly places" (Eph 6:12).

Brett died in October, and from mid-December through the beginning of January, I experienced this. My eyes even felt heavy, and not just from crying. I kept offering it to God as a sacrifice but continually begged him to lift it at the same time because it was so intense and overwhelming. On January 1, I began to write in my prayer journal about this, and by the end of the entry, I was able to praise God for everything for which I was thankful. On January 9, I woke up and it was gone! It felt like a one hundred pound weight was lifted from me. I still felt sad about Brett, but not despair. Because it was a spiritual attack, fighting it with the right weapons (the sacraments and prayer in the form of offering it up, begging God to lift it, thankfulness, and praise) made all the difference in the world.

Anxiety About My Family's Safety

I was constantly in panic mode about the safety of my family. Prior to Brett's death, I had somehow bought into what I call the prosperity Gospel—the belief that each member of my family would be protected and eventually (even automatically) be converted because of my prayers, sacrifices, and fidelity to God's will.

Reality hit with Brett's death, and I realized that God wasn't going to protect them from every single thing just because I was praying. The way my family members use their freedom truly matters, and even if they did that perfectly, suffering still exists and God allows it for a greater good. This was extremely difficult to accept because I felt I had nowhere and no one to lean on for the kind of security that I desperately wanted. I would pray constantly, "Please God, do not allow something like this to happen ever again!"

I knew from my theological studies that there are things that could possibly happen to us, because of the free will choices we or others make, that can be averted through prayer, but there are other things that cannot be averted because they fit into a much bigger plan that God is working out for his glory and the salvation of souls. I was desperately asking God to protect my family from anything else that may fall into that second category.

One day when I was walking my dog and anxiously praying that way, God spoke to my heart. He said, "You know that I cannot promise that to you. But if there is something else like this in your future, I will carry you then, as I am carrying you now."

I didn't hear the words audibly, but the understanding was placed in my heart and with it came a peace that has never left me. Providentially, the following week in our *Walking with Purpose* Bible study lesson, we read the following quote by St. Francis de Sales: "Do not fear what may happen tomorrow; the same everlasting Father who cares for you today will take care of you then and every day. He will either shield you from suffering or will give you unfailing strength to bear it. Be at peace, then, and put aside all anxious thoughts and imaginations." I knew that God was confirming this truth for me!

To my great surprise, my faith is actually stronger now. Before Brett died, I would have never thought I could handle anything like this. Now I trust that God's grace is sufficient for whatever we will go through.

Anxiety About God's Intentions

I was having a rough week right before the first Mother's Day following Brett's death, and I was heading down into a dark place because I was focusing too much on the pain and confusion. I kept asking God questions like, "Why would you let this happen? Why would you let me know about things that seem so insignificant now, and not let me know about something so monumentally important? You had my total, undivided attention. I would have laid my life down for him." I ended up getting very angry at God and turning away from him. Thank the Lord for his mercy in the sacraments and that he sends the right message at just the right time.

On Friday, May 6, I went to the sacrament of Reconciliation and confessed my anger, then I attended Mass and I knew that God was speaking directly to my heart through the Gospel, especially the last sentence. Jesus said to his disciples, "Amen, amen, I say to you, you will weep and mourn, while the world rejoices; you will grieve, but your grief will become joy. When a woman is in labor, she is in anguish because her hour has arrived; but when she has given birth to a child, she no longer remembers the pain because of her joy that a child has been born into the world. So you also are now in anguish. But I will see you again, and your hearts will rejoice, and no one will take your joy away from you. On that day you will not question me about anything" (Jn 16:20–23, NABRE). As soon as those words were proclaimed, a profound peace descended into the deepest places in my soul where all my questions were coming from. The need to know the answer to them all disappeared.

It might seem like a paradox, but I have peace in knowing that I won't fully understand until I die and can see everything from God's perspective. I even feel a strange joy because of this. There are at least two reasons for this. First, not knowing the answers gives me the opportunity to exercise the gift of supernatural faith, which means believing in our Father's loving care for us without understanding his mysterious ways. Making acts of faith like this actually increases our capacity to love and trust God because we are humbling ourselves before his greatness and inscrutable, unsearchable ways, while accepting our status as limited human beings. This opens our hearts more fully and removes obstacles so that God can fill it with his peace and joy.

From a human point of view, it doesn't make sense to have peace and joy in this way, but they are real, nonetheless. The second reason is that the harder something is, the more I have to die to myself, the greater the sacrifice I have to offer to God as intercessory prayer for others. In a strange way, this "darkness" about Brett's tragic death, this not knowing why God allowed it, is a great gift because I can offer it up continually as a living sacrifice. I know I will be eternally grateful for the greater good that God is bringing out of this anguish, and that makes all the difference in the world.

The Teaching on Purgatory

One way in which God expanded my heart through this suffering is by greatly increasing my devotion to the holy souls in purgatory. I prayed for them somewhat regularly before Brett's death, but now, it's a primary part of my everyday life.

After Brett died, it seemed that God was giving me signs that he was saved. I asked a priest if I could count on this, and I have never forgotten his answer. It has helped me tremendously even though it was very difficult to hear at first.

He said that God could have let me know this, and he believed it was true, but it would be considered "private revelation" which is always subject to misinterpretation and even deception from the devil. He then said that the danger is that it could lead me away from helping Brett with my prayers and sacrifices if I presume that, because he is saved, he is automatically in heaven and not in purgatory. Instead, the constant teaching of the Church is that unless a person has "St." in front of his / her name (e.g., St. Juan Diego), we should assume they need our help and continually offer prayers and sacrifices for him / her to aid in their journey to full union with God. Praying for Brett's soul is not incompatible with God letting me know he is saved. It should be the logical next step for a Catholic.

What's more, there can be an exchange of spiritual goods between us and the souls in purgatory. They cannot help themselves (so they actually need our help), but they can intercede for us and they will if we ask them.

The *Catechism of the Catholic Church* states, "Our prayer for them [those who have died] is capable not only of helping them, but also of making their intercession for us effective" (958).

We have experienced many blessings through my son's intercession, and I know that I am helping him too. This is so good for my grieving heart! It gives me something concrete and effective to "do" with my grief. It is also a great incentive to grow in holiness so that my prayers and works become even more fruitful for Brett. "The prayer of a righteous man has great power in its effects" (Jas 5:16).

In my heart, I believe that Brett is in purgatory, and because someone I love so much is there, I want to learn as much about it as I can in order to help him in the best possible way. In hindsight, I can see that God planted this desire in my heart, and he used it to lead me to very important Catholic teachings connected to purgatory, teachings I hadn't taken seriously enough before Brett's death but that I need to understand for the salvation and sanctification of myself and others, especially my family. Two of these teachings are the need for living a life of penance and the gift of indulgences.

Our Need for Penance

For some reason, I presumed that all that was needed to be free of any type of punishment (eternal and temporal) for sin was receiving absolution in the sacrament of Reconciliation. I didn't realize that penance is always necessary to completely wash away the negative effects left behind by my sins. In addition to absolution, penance is a channel of God's grace and is his loving, corrective discipline. Examples of penitential acts are the penance received in confession, voluntary acts of self-denial, heartfelt prayers, devoutly attending Holy Mass, fasting, almsgiving, works of mercy, patient endurance of sufferings, and indulgences. Incorporating these things into our everyday life is a wonderful way to grow in holiness while simultaneously being purified from sinful tendencies.

The Gift of Indulgences

Unfortunately, Brett's death took him by surprise, so he didn't have time to adequately prepare for it through penance. He thought he had many years ahead of him, so he put it off. One way I can help him is by gaining indulgences for him. Indulgences are a great gift of God's mercy. They help to satisfy for the temporal punishment due to sins and can be gained for ourselves or for the souls in purgatory. I know that the Lord led me to this treasure as one of the most effective ways of assisting Brett.

On my part, I try to gain as many indulgences as I can each day and offer them for Brett and all the souls in purgatory. Indulgences offer me a wonderful incentive to make my entire day into a prayer—an offering of love. There are indulgences for specific prayers, for diligently fulfilling our daily duties, and bearing the difficulties of life with a Christian spirit. There are indulgences for acts of charity and/or penance. I try to offer every prayer, work, joy, sorrow, and suffering, every difficultly—traffic, weather, rudeness from other people, difficult situations at work, headaches—as an indulgence by bearing each one patiently and offering them with love to God.

Indulgences are so important because they greatly increase the value of our acts of penance by drawing additional grace from the treasury of the Church which is the treasury of the merits of Jesus Christ and, through him, of Mary and the saints. Indulgences, at the very least, double the value of our acts of love.

I always pray for Brett this way, and then I ask him to pray for specific needs that come up. God often answers those prayers in obvious ways. Through these experiences, God has taught me that my relationship with Brett is ongoing. We are actually creating new memories. I don't have to cling to the past, because we are growing in holiness together and advancing deeper into the heart of God right now.

The following story, from our daughter Nicole's wedding, is a testimony of how God blesses us when we pray for our dead in this way and ask them to intercede for us. We like to call it "Sharing a Coke with Brett."

On the way to the dress rehearsal, Nicole and I asked God to be with us throughout the weekend and to watch over Sam and Nicole in their marriage. We then prayed for the repose of Brett's soul and asked him to intercede for Sam and Nicole and all the needs of the wedding. At the end of the prayer, I asked God to somehow let us know that Brett was doing this and was with us.

During the reception, one of Sam's friends was walking down the hall and noticed the soda machine. At that moment she felt a strong desire to purchase a Coke (even though we were serving them right inside the main room). The Coke she purchased had the words "Share a Coke with Brett"! We had never seen one with his name on it, so we believed it was God's way of letting us know that Brett was with us and was praying for us!

The fruit of his prayers were felt throughout the wedding weekend:

- The weather was perfect! Typically, it's super-hot in early September in Georgia. That weekend it was sunny and in the mid-seventies with virtually no humidity and a very slight breeze. This is a blessing in and of itself, but when you consider that Hurricane Irma hit the next day, it is obvious that there was divine intervention.

- Nicole is a die-hard Michigan Wolverine fan, and this is something that she shared with Brett. That day, they won their football game and Michigan's arch-rival Ohio State lost. It was unusual for both of these to happen on the same day. This might not seem like a big deal, but it truly was for Nicole.

- There was so much peace in the air. Everyone got along so well, even the people who had a history of altercations and had never gotten along.

Detachment and Longing for Heaven

This situation has helped me put many things in perspective and to be detached from things that aren't important in the long run. I live with one foot on earth and one foot in eternity. My longing for heaven is so great now; I can't wait to see Brett again, but I don't want to leave my family here. My deepest desire is to do God's will and to work hard, through my prayers and sacrifices, for the salvation of others, so I need to work even harder at growing in holiness and not allow complacency in any area of my life.

Conclusion

Our faith calls us to trust God in all circumstances. God's ways are often impossible to comprehend, so we must believe in his love without understanding at all. Jesus said to Thomas, "Blessed are those who have not seen and yet believe" (Jn 20:29). Blessed are those who don't understand and trust Jesus anyway! Opening ourselves to God's love and mercy enables us to fully trust in him and personally experience and witness the good that God can bring out of our difficulties, trials, and worst sufferings in life.

Jesus said to St. Faustina, "The graces of my mercy are drawn by means of one vessel only, and that is trust. The more a soul trusts, the more it will receive. Souls that trust boundlessly are a great comfort to me, because I pour all the treasures of my graces into them" (*Diary of St. Faustina*, 1578). Making acts of faith like this opens our souls for God to fill with grace and blessings!

The difficulties in my life, especially the loss of my son and all the pain that I experience from it, have led me into a deeper relationship with God—one that, with his grace and my perseverance, will continue to get stronger. Our Catholic faith, full of treasure and truth, has continuously sustained me in this relationship and has made a life of peace possible, to my great surprise. Maintaining this peace takes effort and a conscious decision each day to put into practice the foundations of my faith. Some days are harder than others, and this is when I remember that I have to continue to "build my house on rock" so that nothing can tear it down.

As Jesus said:

> Every one then who hears these words of mine and does them will be like a wise man who built his house upon the rock; and the rain fell, and the floods came, and the winds blew and beat upon that house, but it did not fall, because it had been founded on the rock. And every one who hears these words of mine and does not do them will be like a foolish man who built his house upon the sand; and the rain fell, and the floods came, and the winds blew and beat against that house, and it fell; and great was the fall of it" (Mt 7:24–27).

Our sufferings, great and small, are our crosses. When we turn to God in trustful surrender while carrying them, his love infuses us with the strength to endure them. God's grace truly is sufficient to see us through anything. Our salvation depends on it. St. Paul summed it up well when he wrote, "For the word of the cross is folly to those who are perishing, but to us who are being saved it is the power of God" (1 Cor 1:18).

Postscript: Terri currently works full time as the Adult Faith Formation Coordinator at Holy Trinity Catholic Church in Peachtree City, Georgia. In 2017, she earned a Bachelor of Arts Degree in Theology from Catholic Distance University and a certificate as a Catholic Spiritual Mentor from the Catholic Spiritual Mentorship Program.

Part III

SUFFERING AND THE PURPOSE OF LIFE

Chapter 9

GROWTH AND SERVICE

Jesus's suffering and death on the cross set an example for us to follow. Jesus truly identified with our plight and he willingly took the burden of our sinful condition upon himself. He showed us the depth of God's love by sharing in our suffering and by offering his life on the cross as an atoning sacrifice for our sins. Jesus's passion and death on the cross is redemptive because it brings reconciliation with our heavenly Father and the promise of eternal life in heaven.[60]

But Jesus did not die on the cross so that we could live comfortable lives. His purposes run much deeper. *Jesus did not come to make our lives easier but to make us holier.* He wants to make us more like himself before he takes us up to heaven.

Life with Christ involves humbly striving, with the help of God's grace and the power of the indwelling Holy Spirit, to accomplish God's purpose for our lives. As such, we may need to prioritize our activities and focus more on those things that align with how God wants us to spend our time. In short, your life is not about you. It is about God and God's purposes for you.

What are God's purposes for our life? Christians believe that God has two primary purposes for each of us in this life, both of which help bring eternal salvation in the next life. Neither of these purposes for our lives has anything to do with seeking fun, fame, or fortune. Nevertheless, these two divinely ordained purposes offer the true potential for finding meaning, fulfillment, and happiness in life. These two primary purposes of life are *to grow* in personal virtue and holiness and *to give* ourselves in loving service of God and others. In other words, we are called to live for God and not for ourselves.

First Primary Purpose of Life: To Grow in Personal Virtue and Holiness

A primary purpose of our life on earth is to allow the grace of God to help us grow in personal virtue and goodness—to become more like Christ. So important are human beings in God's plan of salvation that God himself became one of us in the person of Jesus Christ to help us grow in holiness and have the possibility of eternal life in heaven.

As St. Athanasius of Alexandria put it in the fourth century, "For the Son of God became man so that we might become God."[61] And as the *Catechism of the Catholic Church* makes clear, "All Christians in any state or walk of life are called to the fullness of Christian life and to the perfection of charity. *All are called to holiness*: 'Be perfect, as your heavenly Father is perfect' (Mt 5:48)" (2013, emphasis added).

We all share in the universal call to holiness and holiness is possible for each of us. In fact, it is for this reason that we have been created. All people, of whatever age, are called to seek the holiness and virtue that only God provides.

But we do not become holy overnight. Growth in personal holiness and virtue is the mark of a life well lived and takes a lifetime to cultivate. It is a lifelong process of allowing the power and presence of the Holy Spirit to remove our faults and shortcomings so that we can become perfect as our heavenly Father is perfect. This lifelong process of growing in holiness is called sanctification.

We are invited to live with God eternally and to do so within a community of persons. To be worthy of the invitation and to know that we will be at ease in God's presence, we must have matured to the point that we are sanctified. That means we must be rid of all faults which interfere with our living among God's people.

Growth in personal holiness and spiritual maturity requires intentional commitment. We must consciously want to grow, decide to grow, make an effort to grow, and persist in growing. We need to remain vigilant in avoiding sin and growing in virtue. While this is not easy, several specific suggestions for how to grow in holiness and virtue can be found in chapter 11 of my book *Search No More: The Keys to Truth and Happiness*.

It is not a simple matter to go from being a demanding infant to a mature person who lives for God and others.

This process is not to be taken lightly, but very seriously. Of course, it takes a great deal of effort and determination over an entire lifetime on our part. It is by persevering each day in our ordinary tasks and challenges that we are made holy. We eventually reach whatever we stay committed to achieve.

The good news, however, is that we do not strive alone. Growing in holiness and becoming more like Christ is not produced solely by our own efforts but by intentionally asking and allowing the Holy Spirit to live through us. The Holy Spirit is the source and giver of all holiness.

Committing ourselves to allow the Holy Spirit to shape Christ-like character in us is the foundation for growing in virtue and living out God's love in our actions. As we trust in God's grace and allow the Holy Spirit to work in our lives, we are changed into the likeness of Christ. God is with us and God's grace is sufficient. Through prayer and the sacraments, especially Reconciliation and the Eucharist, God comes to us and helps us grow in holiness.

The Eucharist is spiritual food for spiritual life. The spiritual strength that comes from Holy Communion helps us pray, develop our virtues, and resist temptation. This grace of God in this supernatural food heals our soul and gives us strength for our journey heavenward, as well as bringing peace during times of trouble.

But it is even more than that. It has been said, "We are what we eat." Receiving Holy Communion helps transform us into Christ's likeness because it is Jesus Christ himself—body, blood, soul, and divinity—whom we receive. By thoughtfully participating in the Holy Eucharist, Christ gradually changes our values, our thoughts, our words, and our actions to become more like his own. We become what we receive. This enables us to become a better Christian and a holier person.

Pope Francis provides the following words of encouragement on growing in holiness in his apostolic exhortation *Gaudete Et Exsultate* (*On The Call To Holiness In Today's World*):

> To be holy does not require being a bishop, a priest or a religious. We are frequently tempted to think that holiness is only for those who can withdraw from ordinary affairs to spend much time in prayer. That is not the case. We are all called to be holy by living our lives with love and by bearing witness in everything we do, wherever we find ourselves. Are you called to the consecrated life? Be holy by living out your commitment with joy. Are you married? Be holy by loving and caring for your husband or wife, as Christ does for the Church. Do you work for a living? Be holy by laboring with integrity and skill in the service of your brothers and sisters. Are you a parent or grandparent? Be holy by patiently teaching the little ones how to follow Jesus. Are you in a position of authority? Be holy by working for the common good and renouncing personal gain.

> Let the grace of your baptism bear fruit in a path of holiness. Let everything be open to God; turn to Him in every situation. Do not be dismayed, for the power of the Holy Spirit enables you to do this, and

holiness, in the end, is the fruit of the Holy Spirit
in your life.[62]

God's ultimate goal for our life on earth is not comfort but spiritual development leading to a deeper union
with God. Whenever we forget that spiritual development is one of our primary purposes in life, we can easily
despair and become frustrated by circumstances in our
life. But God has a purpose behind every problem.[63] God
uses these problems to develop our character by drawing
us closer to himself. As stated in the *Catechism*, "The way
of perfection passes by way of the Cross. There is no holiness without renunciation and spiritual battle" (2015).

*For many people, this growth in holiness and virtue
seems to occur most often during the hard times in our lives,
the times of struggle, pain, and suffering.* It is through life's
hardships that we are given the opportunity to develop
our trust in God, to experience God's love for us, and to
grow in character and personal holiness. For in times of
trial, we naturally turn to Jesus and seek God's power and
presence more fully in our lives.

God can transform our trials and suffering into a
beautiful strength of character that produces a hope that
will never disappoint us. As St. Paul wrote, "We rejoice in
our sufferings, knowing that suffering produces endurance, and endurance produces character, and character
produces hope, and hope does not disappoint us, because
God's love has been poured into our hearts through the
Holy Spirit who has been given to us" (Rom 5:3–5).

The Holy Spirit gives hope to all who place their trust
in God. This hope enables Christians to persevere with

confident trust in God even in the face of trials, setbacks, and challenges that come our way. God really does love each of us and wants what is best for us (see Mt 6:25–33). That is why God allows suffering to draw us closer to him and to teach us spiritual truths.

God wants us to embrace the truth that our problems, difficulties, and disappointments are storms on the sea of life that are not meant to sink us but to sanctify us.[64] Each "storm" is an opportunity to grow closer to God. As we grow closer to God, the more we love God. And the more we love God, the more we desire to serve God and others. Then, the more we serve God and others, the more like God we will become in our character, attitudes, and actions.

Picture raw gold as it appears when mined from the earth. It is dull, dark, and clumpy. It does not glitter or shine. Its beauty is only potential. Only after it is melted and poured into a mold does it make beautiful jewelry. In the same way, God carefully allows the trials of this life to be opportunities to "melt me, mold me, make me" more into God's image. As the Old Testament book of Wisdom (3:5–6) states, "Having been disciplined a little, they will receive great good, because God tested them and found them worthy of himself; like gold in the furnace he tried them."

Pope St. John Paul II stated, "Difficulties and sorrows, if accepted out of love, are transformed into a privileged way of holiness, which opens onto the horizons of a greater good, known only to the Lord."[65] He also wrote, "Suffering *must serve for conversion*, that is, *for the rebuilding of goodness* in the subject, who can recognize the divine mercy in this call to repentance. The purpose of penance is to overcome evil, which under different forms lies dormant in man. Its purpose is also to strengthen goodness both in man himself and in his relationships with others and especially with God. It is suffering, more than anything else, which clears the way for the grace which transforms human souls."[66]

Even the ancient pagans knew we learn wisdom through suffering and that moral character gets formed through hardship. Just like swimming against the current makes us stronger, so too in our suffering we are made strong in character. We should constantly keep in mind that every problem is a character-building opportunity, and the more difficult it is, the greater is its character-building potential.[67]

However, this growth in character is not automatic. *Many people become bitter rather than better when faced with suffering.* Adversity can cause us to lose hope and become discouraged, or it can bring us closer to God and God's plans for us. *Adversity, then, can either break us or make us, depending upon our reaction to the situation.*

The Bible speaks many times about how perseverance through trials and suffering is how we attain spiritual maturity and grow in holiness (see Jas 5:7–12; 1 Pt 1:6–7; Rom 5:3–5). St. Paul says this about his suffering, "So we do not lose heart. Though our outer nature is wasting away, our inner nature is being renewed every day. For this slight momentary affliction is preparing for us an eternal weight of glory beyond all comparison, because we look not to the things that are seen but to the things that are unseen; for the things that are seen are transient, but the things that are unseen are eternal" (2 Cor 4:16–18). Wouldn't it be beneficial if everyone facing suffering had a similar eternal perspective and understood the "big picture" as did St. Paul?

Of course, nobody likes to suffer or experience hardships. Yet if we see in these circumstances an enhanced opportunity for personal and spiritual growth, we can benefit immensely and eventually be thankful for all things. May we always remember and take comfort in the fact that *temporal trials are people's path to heavenly holiness.* As stated in the Letter to the Hebrews:

> It is for discipline that you have to endure. God is treating you as sons; for what son is there whom his father does not discipline? If you are left without discipline, in which all have participated, then you are illegitimate children and not sons. Besides this, we have had earthly fathers to discipline us and we respected them. Shall we not much more be subject to the Father of spirits and live? For they disciplined us for a short time at their pleasure, but he disciplines us for our good, that we may share his holiness. For the moment all discipline seems painful rather than pleasant; later it yields the peaceful fruit of righteousness to those who have been trained by it. (12:7–11)

The great St. Thomas Aquinas addressed how our patiently following the example of Jesus in our own suffering can help become more like Christ when he wrote:

If you seek the example of love: Greater love than this no man has, than to lay down his life for his friends. Such a man was Christ on the cross. And if he gave his life for us, then it should not be difficult to bear whatever hardships arise for his sake.

If you seek patience, you will find no better example than the cross. Great patience occurs in two ways: either when one patiently suffers much, or when one suffers things which one is able to avoid and yet does not avoid. Christ endured much on the cross, and did so patiently. . . .

Therefore, Christ's patience on the cross was great. In patience let us run for the prize set before us, looking upon Jesus, the author and perfecter of our faith who, for the joy set before him, bore his cross and despised the shame.

If you seek an example of humility, look upon the crucified one, for God wished to be judged by Pontius Pilate and to die. If you seek an example of obedience, follow him who became obedient to the Father even unto death. For just as by the disobedience of one man, namely, Adam, many were made sinners, so by the obedience of one man, many were made righteous.[68]

As previously discussed, in order to be with God in heaven, we need to be perfect as God is perfect. Suffering often offers the means for us to grow in the holiness and spiritual maturity that prepare us for eternal life in the kingdom of God. Suffering is what helps empty us of ourselves and our natural human obsession with our own desires and forces us to look to God for meaning and for our ultimate relationship with him.

Pope St. John Paul II addressed this in his apostolic letter on suffering, "The witnesses of the Cross and Resurrection were convinced that 'through many tribulations we must enter the Kingdom of God.' In the eyes of the just God, before His judgment, those who share in the suffering of Christ become worthy of this Kingdom. Christ has led us into this Kingdom through His suffering. And also through suffering those surrounded by the mystery of Christ's Redemption *become mature enough* to enter this Kingdom."[69]

Suffering is the pathway to test and strengthen our character and prepare our souls for heaven. Suffering is not to be a source of resentment, anger, or alienation from God. Rather, we are called to accept suffering because it provides opportunities to deepen our holiness and become closer to God. Suffering can be salvific when we join with Christ as part of his body in redeeming others and preparing for the life after earth.

St. John of the Cross wrote about the importance of suffering in growing closer to God:

> Would that people might come at last to see that it is quite impossible to reach the thicket of the riches and wisdom of God except by first entering the thicket of much suffering, in such a way that the soul finds there its consolation and desire. The soul that longs for divine wisdom chooses first, and in truth, to enter the thicket of the cross. . . .

The gate that gives entry into these riches of his
wisdom is the cross; because it is a narrow gate,
while many seek the joys that can be gained through
it, it is given to few to desire to pass through it.[70]

In light of the resurrection of Jesus Christ from the
dead, we do not need to live as though this world is all
there is, that our suffering has no purpose, and that
death has the final say. Rather, we can see our suffering
in this world as a means for growth in personal holiness
and spiritual maturity that is preparing us for something
greater, more permanent, and more splendid—eternal
life with God in heaven.

Further Purification in Purgatory

But what if we do not succeed in fully growing in holiness
while here on earth? The Catholic Church has long held
that purgatory is an additional opportunity for purification from sin and growth in holiness.[71] The word *purgatory* comes from the Latin verb *purgatio*, which means
"to purify or cleanse." To undergo purgation is to be purified or cleansed.

Just as gold is purged of impurities during the refin-
ing process, so we also need to be purified of all that is
sinful or unclean before entering heaven. Between the
sinfulness of this life and the glories of heaven, we must
be made pure. Between death and heaven, there is a
purification.

If we are not perfect saints by the time we die—which
very few of us are—purgatory is how we become fully

ready for heaven. Purgatory is a temporary state of purification for imperfect saints. Once the imperfect saints
are purified, they enter heaven. Everyone in purgatory
will go to heaven. It is not a matter of if but when. As
the *Catechism of the Catholic Church* teaches, "All who
die in God's grace and friendship, but still imperfectly
purified, are indeed assured of their eternal salvation; but
after death they undergo purification, so as to *achieve the
holiness necessary to enter the joy of heaven*. The Church
gives the name Purgatory to this final purification of the
elect, which is entirely different from the punishment of
the damned" (1030–31, emphasis added).

Purgatory is the culmination of the process by which
a human being who has died in the grace of God is made
utterly and completely full of God's goodness and perfectly "conformed to the image of his Son" (Rom 8:29).
This sanctification process starts when we commit our
lives to Jesus Christ. Jesus welcomes anyone who comes
to him by faith (Jn 3:16). But he welcomes us in order to
transform us (Rom 12:2).

Our relationship with Jesus is a cooperative endeavor
in which the Holy Spirit helps us attain the holiness begun
at our baptism. Sanctification will continue, according to
St. Paul, until "he who began a good work in you will
bring it to completion at the day of Jesus Christ" (Phil
1:6).

In short, God does not rest until we are totally purified from sin and made completely holy. If this process is
not finished by the time we die, then God completes it in
purgatory. God transforms us until we are fully at home

in God's divine and holy life. We must become heavenly in order to be at home in heaven.

Purgatory makes sense because a soul cannot just be declared to be clean but must actually be clean before entering heaven. If a sinful soul is merely "covered like snow on a dunghill" by God's grace (as many Protestants believe), its sinful state still exists. It is still unclean.

Purgatory is when all remaining self-love is purged and we are further purified until only the love of God remains. It is when we come to fully realize the love and mercy of God towards us so that we will want to and be fully able to choose only the good in love. Purgatory is when we become, by the grace of God, finally and completely able and willing to use our free will to choose only Love—God himself.

One cannot be in heaven unless one is consumed with love for God. In that, there is no room for sin. In heaven, no one will sin because no one will want to sin. There is no longer any motive to sin in heaven because we will be totally in love with being in the direct presence of the most holy beauty, joy, peace, and love of God—the Supreme and Ultimate Good.

St. Catherine of Genoa was a fifteenth-century mystic who saw purgatory as a process we enter knowing it will lead to God—a stepping stone to heaven.[72] She wrote that the "inner fire" of purgatory is God's love "burning" the soul so that, at last, the soul is wholly aflame with the love of God. It is the pain of wanting to be made totally worthy of being with God, who is pure holiness and goodness. About purgatory, she wrote, "rust which is sin, covers souls, and . . . is burnt away by fire, the more it is consumed, the more the soul responds to God. . . . As the rust lessens and the soul is opened to the divine rays, happiness grows."[73]

The pain of purgatory is the desire for full union with God, which is assured but not yet realized. As stated in the *Handbook for Today's Catholic*, "Having passed through purgatory, you will be utterly unselfish, capable of perfect love. Your selfish ego—the part of you that restlessly sought self-satisfaction—will have died forever. The 'new you' will be your same inner self, transformed and purified by the intensity of God's love for you."[74]

Purgatory is the assurance that there will, in the end, be absolutely nothing to dim the mirror of our lives from fully reflecting the love and goodness of God. Purgatory is when God, the loving and merciful Father, washes his children of all impurity. We, who have been a slave to sin for too long, will be completely released from its power. In purgatory, it is God, the All-Consuming Fire, who lovingly purifies us of our sinful tendencies.

Purgatory, however, is often imagined as a place, but it is actually a condition and a process.[75] Purgatory is the final process of sanctification that most of us will need to undergo before we enter heaven. When our souls have been purified so that we can use them only for the purpose they were created—to perfectly love God and others—we will be ready to enter heaven.

To become more like Christ, we must develop the mind of Christ. That means not thinking so much about our own wants and focusing on the needs of others. This brings us to the second primary purpose in life.

Second Primary Purpose of Life: To Lovingly Serve God and Others

There are two fundamental orientations we can have towards life—either *to get* or *to give*. Many people, especially when younger, mostly want to get from life. Infants can only get things from others to meet their needs. Something about life, however, can enable us to move from being more of a taker to being more of a giver. Whereas an infant naturally seeks to get things from others, how many of us have grandparents who are remarkably self-giving?

The longer we live, the more we realize it is in giving of ourselves in loving service to God and others, and not by seeking our own self-centered gratification, that we find true joy, happiness, and fulfillment. We become fully alive when we actively and lovingly serve God and others.

Thus, the second primary purpose of life is *to serve* by giving our time, talents, and treasure in loving service of God and others. The *Catechism of the Catholic Church* states, "God put us in the world to know, to love, and to serve him, and so to come to paradise" (1721). Giving ourselves in service of God and others should be an essential priority in this life for Christians of any age. If we aren't serving, we're just existing, because life is meant for ministry.[76]

God often allows us to go through suffering and painful experiences to motivate us for ministry with others who are facing similar difficulties. For example, who can better

help an alcoholic than someone who has successfully
dealt with their own alcoholism? And how many cancer
survivors reach out and walk with others who are suffering from cancer with empathy, encouragement, and
compassionate support?

We are often most effective at serving God and others when we use our gifts and abilities in the area of our
strongest interest and in a way that best reflects our own
personality and life experiences—especially our painful
experiences. That is because *our greatest ministry can
come from our greatest hurt.*[77]

As St. Paul wrote, "Blessed be the God and Father of
our Lord Jesus Christ, the Father of mercies and God of
all comfort, who comforts us in all our affliction, so that
we may be able to comfort those who are in any affliction, with the comfort with which we ourselves are com-
forted by God" (2 Cor 1:3–4).

When we serve and help others—especially those
in need, in distress, in pain, or in sorrow—God is using
us as the instrument by which God sends help into the
lives of people. Perhaps a coworker is hurting and needs
someone to listen, or a family member or friend needs
financial help. Each of us can help meet the needs of
someone today and every day. We don't have to do great
things, just "blossom where we are planted."

We manifest and make present the love of God when
we are responsive to the needs of others, as this is when
we show others what God is truly like. With the help of
the Holy Spirit, we are to be a vessel though which God's
love can touch others.

We can lovingly serve God and others through concrete acts of charity on behalf of those in need—the hungry, the homeless, the hurting, the lonely, the imprisoned, the confused, the forgotten. Acts of charity to help meet the physical and bodily needs of others are traditionally called the corporal works of mercy. These include feeding the hungry, giving drink to the thirsty, clothing the naked, offering hospitality to the homeless, caring for the sick, and visiting the imprisoned.

The spiritual works of mercy are another way to actively demonstrate our love by helping others with their spiritual and emotional needs. These works of mercy include counseling the doubtful, educating the uninformed, admonishing the sinner, comforting the sorrowful, forgiving offenses willingly, bearing wrongs patiently, and praying for others. Christian love is the active bearing of another's burden, whether physical, emotional, or spiritual.

We serve God by seeking what God, not me, wants to do with my life. God has a purpose and a plan for each of our lives here on earth. God never tires of helping us find the way to the peace and joy that comes from aligning ourselves with God's will. Our responsibility is to prayerfully discern God's will for our lives and then act accordingly. (Specific guidance for how to discern God's will is discussed in the next chapter.)

As stated by St. John Henry Newman:

> God has created me to do Him some definite service. He has committed some work to me which He has not committed to another. I have my mission.

I may never know it in this life, but I shall be told it in the next. I am a link in a chain, a bond of connection between persons. He has not created me for naught. I shall do good; I shall do His work. I shall be an angel of peace, a preacher of truth in my own place, while not intending it if I do but keep His commandments.

Therefore, I will trust Him, whatever I am, I can never be thrown away. If I am in sickness, my sickness may serve Him, in perplexity, my perplexity may serve Him. If I am in sorrow, my sorrow may serve Him. He does nothing in vain. He knows what He is about. He may take away my friends. He may throw me among strangers. He may make me feel desolate, make my spirits sink, hide my future from me. Still, He knows what He is about.[78]

When we live our everyday lives with a focus on these two purposes—to grow in personal holiness and to lovingly serve God and others—we become fully alive and our life becomes an offering to God. As the Danish proverb says, "*What you are is God's gift to you, what you become is your gift to God.*"[79]

The following classic poem expresses how we are called to repay—with the deepest gratitude—our profound debt to God for his many gifts and blessings (even the trials) in this life and in the eternal life to come:

> *I'd like to think when life is done*
> *That I had filled a needed post,*
> *That here and there I'd paid my fare*

With more than idle talk and boast;
That I had taken gifts divine,
The breath of life and manhood fine,
And tried to use them now and then
In service for my fellow men.

I'd hate to think when life is through
That I had lived my round of years
A useless kind, that leaves behind
No record in this vale of tears;
That I had wasted all my days
By treading only selfish ways,
And that this world would be the same
If it had never known my name.

I'd like to think that here and there,
When I am gone, there shall remain
A happier spot that might have not
Existed had I toiled for gain;
That some one's cheery voice and smile
Shall prove that I had been worth while;
That I had paid with something fine
My debt to God for life divine.[80]

Chapter 10

DISCERNING GOD'S WILL

This is a letter Steve Hemler wrote to family and friends in April 1998 after starting a new job in Saudi Arabia and shortly before his wife, Linda, and children, Jonathan, Christopher, and Allison, joined him there. His hope and prayer in sharing this difficult yet affirming experience is that it will help others discern God's will in their lives, including during hard times.

I am writing this letter because you may be wondering how my family and I came to believe that moving to Saudi Arabia was God's will for us. Please do not think I share this out of some "holier-than-thou" or self-righteous attitude. Heaven forbid. Rather, I share this testimony out of a humble and sincere hope that our experience may be of some help to you in your life as a Christian disciple.

Furthermore, I hope sharing our conviction that moving to Saudi Arabia is God's will for us will help you to not be worried or concerned about us over here. As it says in the Bible, "We know that in everything God works for good with those who love him, who are called according to his purpose" (Rom 8:28).

Trying to correctly discern God's will in the decision to move to Saudi Arabia was of the utmost importance to us. However, trying to correctly discern God's will in any decision, especially one as significant as moving one's entire family to the Middle East, is often quite difficult.

Of course, our whole family prayed a lot. We reflected and read Scripture for guidance. We discussed the matter with friends and relatives. And we found a book by Fr. Michael Scanlan, president of Franciscan University of Steubenville, most helpful. This book, which I purchased on a business trip to Portland, Oregon, just last April, is entitled *What Does God Want: A Practical Guide to Making Decisions.*[81]

In this short book, Fr. Scanlan shares five tests which, when prayerfully applied in a spirit of submission to the Lord and openness to the Holy Spirit, are invaluable in helping discern God's will. *These five tests are the conformity, conversion, confirmation, consistency, and conviction tests.*

However, before I share our application of these five tests to the decision to move to Saudi Arabia, please allow me to recap the events leading up to this decision. My employer since 1981, Eastman Chemical Company in Kingsport, Tennessee, had publicly announced and had begun implementing a program to reduce sustained costs (including labor) by 500 million dollars by the year 2000.

In August 1997, I was told by my new department head that Eastman had too many civil engineers. Ever since Eastman began contracting out all detailed design,

I believed this to be the case too. I never could understand how it was best for Eastman to contract all detailed design and then keep all their design engineers. Clearly, the handwriting was on the wall.

Fortunately, through my involvement in three industry-wide consortiums, I had gotten to know many engineers who worked at other companies. A couple of years ago, I remember casually discussing with two engineers who worked for the Saudi Arabian Oil Company (also known as Saudi Aramco or Aramco, for short) about their life in Saudi Arabia. I remember being intrigued by the adventure and lifestyle. At that time, however, I never gave moving to Saudi Arabia one moment's serious consideration.

Nevertheless, in September 1997, I mailed my resume to several engineers I knew who worked at other companies (including Saudi Aramco), since I felt my job was insecure at Eastman. On the first of October, I was asked by Aramco to come for an interview in Houston the following week.

On Saturday, October 4, Christopher, Jonathan, and I attended the outstanding and spiritually uplifting Promise Keeper's "Stand In The Gap" sacred assembly of nearly a million men in Washington, DC. On Monday, October 6, I flew from Kingsport to Houston and interviewed with Aramco.

About a week later, I faxed a letter to Aramco with specific information about the annual bonuses I had previously received from Eastman. In that fax, I stated that any offer from Aramco must be competitive with my total compensation (including these bonuses) in order for me to consider joining Aramco. I would never have said that had I known what was to happen next.

For on October 23, 1997, I lost my job at Eastman. As you can imagine, suddenly and involuntarily losing one's job of seventeen years is quite traumatic.

The next several weeks were a real difficult time. Was I going to fall into bitterness, despair, and worry? Or was I going to really believe that God could be calling us to a new life and to truly trust that God would provide for our family? This was a real struggle, a real struggle.

I struggled with truly accepting and believing the words of Jesus about worry from the Sermon on the Mount (Mt 6:25–34). I also struggled to accept these words of Fr. Scanlan, "The essence of our relationship with God is one of trust. He will care for us. He will give us the grace for the moment—not for all possible future moments. He gives us grace to begin our walk with him. We are to have trust that He will give us the grace for every circumstance—foreseen and unforeseen—along that path. This is the most important application of the consistency test. It is more crucial to be consistently trusting in God's love and grace than in anything else."[82]

Finally, after a month of internal struggle, prayer, reflection, reading, and discussion, and mostly by the grace of God, I was finally able to let go of my worry and despair and trust in God. I was given a real peace. I came to truly believe this challenge was a special opportunity for our entire family to *really* trust in God and seek his will even more deeply than we ever had before.

Of course, I cannot even begin to express how much the support, encouragement, understanding, and advice

of my wonderful wife, Linda, meant to me. Her stead-
fast love and support made all the difference during this
very difficult period of my life. I am so thankful for being
gifted with such a terrific wife.

Interestingly, the week *before* we received the job
offer from Aramco, I told Linda I "knew" when it would
arrive (even though we had not yet heard anything from
Aramco about a forthcoming offer). *I told her the offer
would arrive the following week, on Tuesday, December 2.
She asked how I knew that! I said, "Because December 2
is exactly forty days and forty nights after I lost my job at
Eastman."*

*Well, when I saw the FedEx truck pull up in front of
our house on December 2, I fell on my knees on our living
room floor and offered God a heartfelt prayer of gratitude
and thanksgiving. The driver then delivered the Aramco
job offer.* Even though I previously went on a couple of
other interviews, I never did receive any other job offers.

Since we had been seeking God's will, our decision to
accept Aramco's job offer was already made by the time it
arrived. As I stated earlier, we found the five tests for dis-
cerning God's will in Fr. Scanlan's book *What Does God
Want?* to be most helpful. Again, these five tests are the
conformity, conversion, confirmation, consistency, and
conviction tests. This is how we prayerfully evaluated
each of these "five C's" regarding our family's move to
Saudi Arabia.

Five Tests for Discerning God's Will

First, the *conformity test*. Fr. Scanlan states, "The conformity test asks us to compare our proposed decision, commitment, journey, or action to the will of God for His people as revealed in scripture, tradition, and the authoritative teaching of the Church."[83]

This one was easy. We did not see any conflict with God's revealed will or Church teaching in moving to Saudi Arabia. We found nothing sinful about moving there. Rather, we saw it as a real learning adventure, especially for our children. This would be a unique opportunity to experience more of God's creation, places, and cultures.

The second test, the *conversion test*, asks, "Will the proposed action draw us closer to God or lead us away from Him? In one sense the test of conversion is the only one that matters. The whole point of the Christian life is to love God and to prepare ourselves to be with Him for eternity. . . . However, holiness doesn't descend on us like a cloud of glory from heaven. We grow in it, through trouble and challenge, over obstacles and opposition—by God's grace."[84]

This is key. I can truly say that this whole experience has brought and continues to bring me much closer to God. I also believe it has brought my entire family closer together and closer to God.

Clearly, the forty-day period of uncertainty between jobs was a time of purification and preparation. As I previously shared, this was a time of personal struggle between falling into worry and despair or coming to truly trust in God.

It is interesting how many times the number forty occurs throughout the Bible as encompassing a period of purification and preparation, a time of learning to trust and depend more fully on God. For example, the rains fell on Noah's Ark for forty days and forty nights (Gn 7:12). Moses stayed on Mt. Sinai for forty days and forty nights before bringing down the tablets of the Ten Commandments (Ex 34:28). The Israelites wondered in the desert for forty years, and had their faith tested many times, after escaping from slavery in Egypt (Dt 29:5). The first major prophet, Elijah, walked forty days and forty nights to the mountain of God, Horeb (1 Kgs 19:8). Jesus fasted and was tempted in the desert for forty days just before beginning his public ministry (Mk 1:12–13). Jesus's ascension into heaven was forty days after his resurrection (Acts 1:3).

This is the reason that Lent is forty days long. Lent is the Church's traditional season of purification and preparation, anticipating the sorrow of Good Friday and the joy of Easter Sunday.

During my forty-day period of purification and preparation between jobs, I had more than my normal amount of time available for prayer, reading, and reflection. I particularly felt called to use this time, and my time here now, to continue to try to grow in Christian humility and to more truly trust in God's care. Involuntarily losing one's job sort of forces one to become more humble.

I often found and continue to find the words of Mother Teresa on a daily flip calendar we kept by our home computer to be quite meaningful. On September 27, 1997, I purchased this little flip calendar in Knoxville while attending Allison's godmother's wedding. For example, Mother Teresa's reflection for October 28 (five days after I lost my job) was, "Let us all try to practice humility and meekness. We learn humility through accepting those things which make us feel it. Do not let a chance pass you by. It is so very easy to be proud, harsh, moody, and selfish—so easy. But we have been created for greater things; why stoop down to things that will spoil the beauty of our hearts?"

And on October 29, "Humility always radiates the greatness and glory of God. How wonderful are the ways of God! He used humility, smallness, helplessness, and poverty to prove to the world that he loved the world. Let us not be afraid to be humble, small, and helpless to prove our love to God."

I have also found the Promise Keepers' daily Scripture reading and reflection program—in the New Testament given out at "Stand In The Gap"—to be quite beneficial. Many of these daily reflections focus on humility. For example, "Arrogance, pride, and demand for leadership disqualifies one to lead. Yet humility and service establishes leadership. Christ did not demand leadership. Yet throngs of people followed him, as he spent his earthly life serving."

Also, "In our 'I'll do it my way' society, it takes courage to overcome the tendency to think your way is best. Let it be said of you that, in your life, you chose to do it not your way, but God's way, and that you were obedient. Humility creates the environment for obedience."

And from St. Paul in Philippians 2:3, "Do nothing from selfishness or conceit, but in humility count others better than yourselves." There are many other Scripture passages that encourage Christian humility (e.g., Col 3:12; Eph 4:2; 1 Pt 5:5–7; Jas 3:13–18, and of course the Beatitudes in Mt 5:3–12).

Not only have I used this opportunity to try to become more humble in spirit, but I have also tried to develop a consistent trust in God. Coincidentally, Mother Teresa's daily reflection for October 18 (only five days *before* I lost my job) was, "Total surrender means totally abandoning ourselves into His hands; yielding totally to His every movement of love, giving Him supreme freedom over us to express His love as He pleases, with no thought of self."

And her words for the next day, October 19, were, "Loving trust means an absolute, unconditional, and unwavering confidence in God our loving Father, even when everything seems to be a total failure; to look to Him alone as our help and protector, trusting to the point of rashness with courageous confidence in his fatherly goodness." How appropriate for what was to happen in only a more few days. Praise be to our Father in heaven!

God continues to provide help in my ongoing effort to grow in Christian humility and trust. For example, when we returned home after visiting friends and relatives over the Christmas holidays, the January 1998 edition of the Catholic magazine *Liguorian* was in our stack of mail. Interestingly, this magazine, which we received exactly one month to the day before I was to leave for

Steve Hemler

Saudi Arabia, has a picture of a desert on the cover with the title "The Desert: Landscape of Grace." This article was the first in a yearlong series of articles on how "the desert has much to teach us about spiritual transformation and the meaning of our faith." Imagine that!

This monthly series continues to have especially pertinent reflections for our lives in Saudi Arabia. For example, when the Jews left the slavery of Egypt and wondered into the desert, "it meant relinquishing a familiar security and embarking on a life of radical dependence upon God. It meant exchanging the known for the unknown."

And from the March article in this series on desert spirituality, "I gradually came to understand one of the most important things the desert had to teach me: to enter the desert is to relinquish the illusion of control. I am referring to the habits of fear and control that keep us from giving ourselves completely to God."

I certainly believe this call to relinquish familiar security and embark on a life of radical dependence upon God is also our call and our challenge, especially in moving to Saudi Arabia. In this we try to follow in the footsteps of many people in the Bible who spent time in the desert, including Abraham, Moses, John the Baptist, and St. Paul. Even Jesus himself spent forty days and nights in the desert before commencing his ministry.

I truly believe living in Saudi Arabia provides additional opportunities to learn to trust ever more deeply in God. For example, the various threats to the peace in the Middle East (e.g., Iraq) provide an opportunity for increased trust in God. However, even if something unforeseen should happen, this whole experience has taught us much about the spiritual growth value of difficulty and hardship.

Living in Saudi Arabia cannot help but bring us closer to God. As you know, public practice of any faith other than Islam is forbidden in Saudi Arabia. However, this makes whatever options are permitted all the more precious. Everything that is easy to take for granted elsewhere becomes all the more precious here because it could be taken away at any time. Clearly, one's commitment to the faith becomes much greater when the practice of one's faith cannot be taken for granted.

I have gotten involved in the Catholic community here and believe my family will too. There are several organized opportunities to grow in faith. For instance, I never would have attended a weekly men's prayer breakfast at 5:30 a.m. before!

Furthermore, this is a very religious society. The Islamic daytime fasting during the entire month of Ramadan, the annual Hajj pilgrimage, and the public call to prayer five times a day constantly remind us of God. I have even begun pausing for private prayer whenever I hear the Arabic call to prayer chanted several times a day from loudspeakers at the mosques. If Muslims can regularly pray that often every day, we Christians can too!

The next test, the *confirmation test*, asks us to seek confirmation that our decisions are indeed God's will. Decisions are often confirmed through the unfolding of favorable circumstances that make the decision possible. Fr. Scanlan writes, "Often circumstances will provide confirmation; doors will open, resources become available, possibilities turn into solid realities. Some decisions are confirmed after the fact as we see the fruit they bring. Occasionally, the Lord will confirm a decision through signs and wonders. . . . Always look at circumstances with the eyes of faith. . . . The natural appearance of these events can cause us to miss their spiritual significance. Their significance comes from their context."[85]

Many of the circumstances and "coincidences" of this whole experience, when viewed through the "eyes of faith," sure seem to confirm that it is God's will for us to move to Saudi Arabia. The first "coincidence" was the timely loss of my job at Eastman. I can tell you without a doubt that I never, ever would have accepted any offer from Aramco (no matter how much money they offered) if I was still employed at Eastman. I never, ever could have voluntarily left such a good place to live (Kingsport) or personally initiated such hardship on my family (moving to a foreign country). I never, ever could have been the one totally responsible for my children having to leave all their friends, relatives, and the only home they've ever known.

It is a plain and simple fact that if I was to ever accept a job in Saudi Arabia, I first needed to be no longer employed at Eastman. The timing was "perfect" too. If I had lost my job even a week earlier, I would certainly not have pressed the bonus issue with Aramco (which delayed their offer). If much later, I likely would have already turned down their offer, which was valid for only ten days.

Yes, it all happened in such a timely manner that I believe it just had to be part of God's plan and purpose. I was meant to lose my job at Eastman exactly forty days before being offered a much better job at Saudi Aramco. Call it silly or weird. Or call it the "eyes of faith." However, I am convinced this was God's will for myself and my family.

A second "coincidence" is the tremendous relevance and meaning of Mother Teresa's words on our daily flip calendar, especially five days before and five days after I lost my job. Even her words for October 23 are relevant and comforting to a person who just lost his job and means of providing for his family, "We must drink deeply from the very Source the deep calm and peace of interior quietude and refreshment of God, allowing the pure water of divine grace to flow plentifully and unceasingly from the Source itself."

A third "coincidence" was the fact that I foresaw—and indeed it happened—that the job offer from Aramco arrived exactly forty days after I lost my job at Eastman. This "deliverance" from my period of purification and preparation was at the "biblically correct" time! Seriously,

I find the significance of that forty-day timing hard to ignore.

A fourth "coincidence" was the Scripture reading and homily at the small daily Mass I attended on Wednesday, December 3—the day after I received the job offer from Aramco. During the entire time I was unemployed, I attended Mass at our children's Catholic school every Wednesday morning.

Every children's Mass I attended, except the one on December 3, was held in the gym at St. Dominic Catholic School. For some reason, the Mass this day was instead held in the quaint chapel at St. Dominic Church. Dr. Frank Fisher (another close friend, confidant, and advisor during this whole affair) and I drove our cars from the school to the church for Mass this Wednesday morning.

Upon entering the chapel, I was asked by a lady I barely knew if I'd like to read the Scripture readings. This was also unusual because the children always read the Scripture readings for every Mass held at their school. I don't remember what the first reading was, but as I was reading the Responsorial Psalm, I nearly cried.

Here I was, the day after my "deliverance," reading out loud at Mass the words of Psalm 23 ("The LORD is my shepherd, I shall not want."). I have never felt the power and meaning of those beautiful words so personally before. Nor have I ever been so grateful to God for his tender love and care.

Then Fr. Tom (who was totally unaware of my discussions with Saudi Aramco) shared during his homily that this day (December 3) was the feast day of St. Francis

Xavier, the patron saint of foreign missions. Frank and I looked at each other unbelievingly.

Fr. Tom continued that St. Francis Xavier, one of the founders of the Jesuit religious order, had traveled extensively throughout the Middle East, India, China, Japan, etc. preaching the Good News. While I do not feel called to preach, I do find the conviction, courage, and willingness of St. Francis Xavier to follow God's call into foreign lands quite inspiring.

A fifth "coincidence," as previously mentioned, was the cover article on desert spirituality in the January *Liguorian* magazine, which we received exactly one month to the day before I left for Saudi Arabia. This yearlong series is so relevant to life here that I have been asked to share each month's article at the men's prayer breakfast I regularly attend.

Now I'd like to consider another test of God's will, the *consistency test*. In the words of Fr. Scanlan, the consistency test asks:

> Does the option we are considering seem to fit the kind of person we are? Is it consistent with the way God has worked with us in the past? Has the Lord ever spoken to us this way before? . . . We will often find Him following a plan that unfolds over a period of years. . . . In fact, the current possibility under consideration may be part of the unfolding of a larger plan that the Lord has previously set in motion and which you have already determined to be His will. If so, your decision-making may be very

simple. All you need to do is determine whether
the current direction is part of a larger plan."[86]

I can say without a doubt that God has worked like
this with me before by providing "coincidences" that seem
to confirm a course of action. In 1989, I felt a strong call
to get involved in pro-life work and continued to marvel
at how God blessed our many educational and political
efforts in northeast Tennessee. I had also written an article promoting a "vital signs of life" (heartbeat and brain
activity) abortion public policy proposal.[87] One morning
in January 1990, I stopped at the post office on my way
to work to submit this article for publication for the first
time in a national magazine. When I walked out of the
post office, there was a big, beautiful rainbow in the sky.
As I drove to work, I continued to marvel at this beautiful rainbow centered right over the road. When I got to
work and was walking into the office, I was still looking
up marveling at this rainbow. However, I stopped dead
in my tracks when I suddenly realized this rainbow had
appeared exactly when I was inside the post office mail-
ing my article for publication the first time. I could not
believe the amazing "coincidence" of the appearance of
this rainbow and took it as an encouraging sign to persevere in my efforts.

Unsurprisingly, this article was rejected by *National
Review* and other magazines over several years. Nevertheless, I continued to persevere, including joining with
a law professor and a medical doctor as co-authors. After
repeated submittals, *National Review* finally accepted
this article for publication, but only after I faxed them

ALLEN. Opposes waiting period for handgun buyers. Though he is against the new law limiting handgun purchases, he would not repeal the measure. Allen said a woman should be allowed to have an abortion until the point in the pregnancy when there is medical evidence of a heartbeat or brain activity.

REEL LUCKY Third-grader Danny Ferk, a four-year fishing veteran, lugs in a whopper of a bass with his 'lucky pole'— the perfect ending for an old story. **Sports, C1.**

an article about Virginia gubernatorial candidate George Allen espousing the same position that was printed on the front page of a Tidewater Virginia newspaper.[88] What is really striking is the only reason I purchased that Sunday newspaper while visiting relatives in Williamsburg— and ever saw the George Allen article—was because a photo I took of my seven-year-old nephew with a citation bass he had just caught was also printed on the front page. I still find it amazing that the only reason this article was published in *National Review*[89] and later reprinted in *The Human Life Review*[90] was because of a big fish! Yes, these "coincidences" have happened before in my life.

Furthermore, I do believe our move to Saudi Arabia is part of God's unfolding plan for each person in our family. I, for example, have long felt called to full-time Christian ministry. However, I have been concerned about how I would meet my financial responsibilities to my family with such a relatively low paying job. Will the money we can now save permit me to move into full-time Christian ministry and still be able to support my family? Probably.

This is a calling I intend to pursue. During my annual month-long repatriation trips, I intend to complete the additional three courses I need to obtain a master's degree in pastoral studies from Loyola University in Chicago. Over the past twelve years, I've managed to obtain twenty-three of the required thirty credits for this degree, which is a good prerequisite for lay ministry in the Catholic Church.

(I obtained that Master's degree from Loyola in January 2002, and in 2011, I voluntarily took early retirement as soon as I could from Saudi Aramco in order to follow this calling to serve God and the Church full time, primarily through the ministry of the Catholic Apologetics Institute of North America. For more on this ministry, see: www.cainaweb.org.)

I do not claim to know all the reasons why God seems to have called us to move to Saudi Arabia or what God has planned for Linda, Jonathan, Christopher, Allison, and me. We'll just have to wait and see how things "play out" over time. Only then will we fully know why God apparently wants us all here. Until then, we'll just have to trust in God and make the most of all our opportunities for growth in Christian discipleship and service—one day at a time.

Of the fifth test, the *conviction test*, Fr. Scanlan writes, "The final test of a decision is the inner conviction that this course of action is indeed the right one. The first four tests emphasize the making up of the mind. . . . Conviction is the test of the heart. Do we 'know' inside that this is the right way? . . . We need to pay special attention to the difference between peace in the heart and conclusion of the mind. The two should both be present in a major decision, but they are not the same thing."[91]

Another easy one. We believe this move to Saudi Arabia is God's will and will be a very good experience for all of us. We are excited about the learning adventure and travel that this new international lifestyle will provide. We look forward to additional challenges to help us grow in our faith, in our Christian service, and in our trust in God for everything—as we follow the unfolding of God's plan for each person in our family. We are grateful for this unique opportunity.

After prayerfully applying the conformity, conversion, confirmation, consistency, and conviction tests to find out what God wants us to do, we can confidently venture forth in faith and step out in courage, knowing that God's grace is sufficient. For as Christians, we are called to walk by faith and not by fear.

Chapter 11

THE ANSWERER

The answer to the problem of suffering is not just an abstract idea, because this is not just an abstract issue. It is a personal issue and requires a personal response. The answer to the problem of suffering is not a logical answer, but an Answerer.[92] The Answerer is Jesus Christ himself. God understands our suffering because he has experienced it.

Although God, Jesus became fully human and experienced life just as we do. He was tempted as we are. He dealt with grief, sadness, and rejection. He also felt joy and happiness, as well as shared intimate moments with close friends. The only thing Jesus did not experience was sin. But because Jesus paid the price for sin, he experienced the suffering of sin's consequences.

As Christians, we must go where Jesus is, and the cross is one of the places where he is. By dying on the cross, Jesus did not obliterate human suffering. Rather, he embraced it. By his suffering, Jesus shares in our own suffering. He knows and understands our pain and suffering. Mother Teresa knew this well and shared, "Pain, sorrow, suffering are but the kiss of Jesus—a sign that you have come so close to Him that He can kiss you."[93]

Whenever we think that no one understands or cares, we should remember that Jesus definitely does because he has been there too. God, in Jesus Christ, understands what we are going through because he has been through it himself. True compassion not only identifies and empathizes with the one who is in pain but takes that pain upon oneself in order to bring help and restoration. That is what Jesus does for us. As the Letter to the Hebrews states, "For because he himself has suffered and been tempted, he is able to help those who are tempted" (Heb 2:18).

Are we broken? Jesus was broken like bread for us. Are we despised? He was despised and rejected. Do people betray us? Jesus himself was sold out. Are our relationships damaged? He too loved and was rejected. Are we in pain? Jesus experienced much pain himself. What more can he do?

How can we not help but love in return this person, Jesus, who went the extra mile for us, who voluntarily entered into our world, who suffered our pains, and who offers himself to us in the midst of our own pain and suffering? Christians find comfort and support knowing that Jesus fully understands our suffering because he himself suffered during his time on earth. Jesus willingly unites his cross in solidarity with our own.

God entered fully into our human condition in the person of Jesus Christ, who willingly suffered for our good so that we might attain eternal salvation in heaven. As the one mediator between God and man, Jesus offers forgiveness of sins and a living, eternal relationship with God to all who choose to turn from their self-centered lives and commit themselves to him as their Lord and Savior. As stated in the Letter to the Hebrews, "Although he was a Son, he learned obedience through what he suffered; and being made perfect he became the source of eternal salvation to all who obey him" (Heb 5:8–9).

Bishop Kevin Rhoades of the Diocese of Fort Wayne-South Bend addressed this in a homily on the meaning and value of suffering:

> The question of the meaning of suffering, in many ways an impenetrable question, finds an answer, above all, in the Passion of Jesus. On the cross, Jesus not only embraced human suffering in an incomparable way, but also made suffering redemptive. He conquered evil with good. He accomplished our salvation from sin and death by His own suffering on the cross. In suffering voluntarily and innocently, Christ gives the answer to the question about suffering and its meaning.
>
> Jesus brings suffering into what we can call "a new dimension," the dimension of love, salvific love. The Son of God strikes evil at its very root, conquering sin and death with the power of love. "He conquers sin by His obedience unto death, and He overcomes death by His resurrection" (*Salvifici Doloris* 14). In His passion, Jesus took all human suffering upon Himself. He gave it a new meaning. He used suffering to accomplish the work of salvation. He used it for good. His love transformed

222   CATHOLIC STORIES OF FAITH AND HOPE

suffering so that this awful reality that is connected
to evil might become a power for good. So suffering now has a saving power. And that is how we,
as Christians, can find meaning and purpose in
suffering, what before we might have thought was
totally useless.[94]

The realization that Jesus truly does love me and
desires my love in return is the only real answer to the
problem of evil and suffering. As evidenced by his atoning sacrifice on the cross, Jesus demonstrated how the
very worst thing that ever happened in the history of the
world ended up resulting in the very best thing that ever
happened in the history of the world. And if it happened
there—the ultimate evil resulting in the ultimate good—
it can also happen in our own individual lives.

God is not a distant force permitting pain from
beyond the clouds.[95] How could God have shown his
love and mercy towards us any more clearly than by taking on our human condition? What better proof could
God have given of his love? The Incarnation shows us
how much God cares for each of us. We do well when we
stop focusing on our own suffering and remember how
much Jesus suffered for our sake and all that he has done
and continues to do for us. God is a personal God who
understands and shares in our suffering and is able to
bring good out of it if we turn to God in hope and trust.

Indeed, we need Jesus Christ as our Savior, not just
as a teacher. If he is only a teacher, then we can read his
words in the Gospels anytime we want and glean things
from him, just like any other teacher. Jesus, however, has

done much more than teach—he rescued us and saved us
from the consequences of our sins. If someone is trapped
in quicksand, they do not need a teacher—they need a
savior.

Until we personally feel what it means to be helpless and vulnerable, we will not appreciate who Jesus is
and what he offers to us. To truly appreciate Jesus Christ
as our Savior, we often have to be brought to the place
where we acutely feel the need for him. As discussed in
the first chapter, suffering has the power to do just that.

How often do we truly come to know Jesus through
our pain and suffering? It is often when we grow tired
from trying to avoid our pain and suffering that we finally
fall to our knees and pray. We then discover that Jesus
was waiting for us all along and it may have been our
resistance and pride that was keeping us from him. Jesus
is eager to receive us and redeem us. He will give meaning to our suffering and heal many of our afflictions. He
knows our hearts and the depths of our yearnings. He
sees us as we truly are and loves us deeply.

It is sometimes assumed that those who follow Jesus
will have relatively easy lives and be free of suffering.
However, there is nothing in the Bible or in the tradition of the Church that should lead us to expect this will
be the case. Being a follower of Jesus, however, does not
mean we will be safe from suffering or hardship, nor
will we be healed of every disease. Jesus did not come to
guarantee us health, wealth, or prosperity. The *Catechism*
speaks to this:

Moved by so much suffering Christ not only allows himself to be touched by the sick, but he makes their miseries his own: "He took our infirmities and bore our diseases." But he did not heal all the sick. His healings were signs of the coming of the Kingdom of God. They announced a more radical healing: the victory over sin and death through his Passover. On the cross Christ took upon himself the whole weight of evil and took away the "sin of the world," of which illness is only a consequence. By his passion and death on the cross Christ has given a new meaning to suffering: it can henceforth configure us to him and unite us with his redemptive Passion. (1505)

The radical difference is that Christians know that Jesus is with us today to help us, comfort us, and encourage us, especially in the midst of suffering. As Jesus promised, "I am with you always" (Mt 28:20). Bishop Robert Barron addresses this in his daily Gospel reflection on Matthew 8:23–7, which is about Jesus calming the storm on the Sea of Galilee:

During the storm, Jesus' disciples cried out to the Lord in desperation: "O Lord, we are drowning; don't you care?" Perhaps there are some people reading this right now who feel themselves in this precise situation. Perhaps you're reading these words from your hospital bed where you are recovering painfully from surgery, or where you've just received some devastating news. Perhaps you find yourself caught in a terrible, unrelenting depression. Maybe you've just lost a loved one, and you're awash in a sea of grief.

If that's you, then pray as the disciples did. Awaken someone who can help. Jesus sleeping in the midst of the storm is a very powerful symbol of God's sovereignty over even the darkest and most difficult trials that life throws at us.

Pope Francis also made this point during his extraordinary urbi et orbi blessing while praying for an end to the coronavirus pandemic:

Faith begins when we realize we are in need of salvation. We are not self-sufficient; by ourselves we founder: we need the Lord, like ancient navigators needed the stars. Let us invite Jesus into the boats of our lives. Let us hand over our fears to him so that he can conquer them. Like the disciples, we will experience that with him on board there will be no shipwreck. Because this is God's strength: turning to the good everything that happens to us, even the bad things. He brings serenity into our storms, because with God life never dies.

The Lord asks us and, in the midst of our tempest, invites us to reawaken and put into practice that solidarity and hope capable of giving strength, support and meaning to these hours when everything seems to be floundering. The Lord awakens so as to reawaken and revive our Easter faith. We have an anchor: by his cross we have been saved. We have a rudder: by his cross we have been redeemed. We have a hope: by his cross we have been healed and

embraced so that nothing and no one can separate
us from his redeeming love.[96]

The Lord Jesus Christ never leaves us alone. He keeps
careful watch over us at all times, especially when we feel
powerless or helpless. Jesus is here with us, even today, to
share in our pain and suffering. He will never leave us.

As St. Paul wrote, "Who shall separate us from the
love of Christ? Shall tribulation, or distress, or persecu-
tion, or famine, or nakedness, or peril, or sword? . . . No,
in all these things we are more than conquerors through
him who loved us. For I am sure that neither death, nor
life, nor angels, nor principalities, nor things present,
nor things to come, nor powers, nor height, nor depth,
nor anything else in all creation, will be able to separate
us from the love of God in Christ Jesus our Lord" (Rom
8:35, 37–39).

Jesus will free us from the anxiety and insecurity that
often arise from suffering and hardship if we but trust in
his loving care and rest securely in his loving friendship.
Jesus assures us that we do not have to give into fear or
discouragement if we place our trust and hope in him
and remember his great love for us.

We can either face the trials and difficulties of this
life alone or we can face them with Jesus. Knowing that
Jesus is with us transforms us and our struggles. Trusting
in the love and care of Jesus when everything around us
seems to be falling apart is the best path to true peace of
mind. Christians know that God is with us, not to necessarily remove us from these hardships, but rather to help

us face them with courage and hope. As stated in a daily
Scripture reflection in *The Word Among Us*:

> Jesus doesn't just tell us not to be afraid; he enters
> into our situation and will remain with us every
> step of the way. This might not mean an instanta-
> neous healing of cancer or a surprise check appear-
> ing in our mailbox. But it may well entail the Lord
> offering you his help just when you most need it.
> Maybe he leads you to an excellent doctor. Maybe
> you learn about a promising new job opportunity.
> Or maybe nothing appears to happen at all, but you
> experience a sense of peace in the midst of turmoil.
> Whatever happens, Jesus wants to show you that he
> is with you for the long haul. He has no intention
> of abandoning you. This means you can trust him,
> even in the most terrifying of storms.[97]

Jesus asks us to trust him in all things, especially
during our trials and suffering. When we are troubled
and in distress, we can turn to Jesus in confidence that he
will be with us. If we trust in Jesus, he will strengthen and
comfort us during times of hardship and suffering. He
will see us through any calamity or trial that comes our
way. The Lord Jesus offers us a supernatural peace and
joy that enables us to bear any sorrow and endure any
pain. As Jesus said, "I have said this to you, that in me you
may have peace. In the world you have tribulation; but
be of good cheer, I have overcome the world" (Jn 16:33).

If we truly trust in Jesus, he will help us bear our
suffering with a deep peace and real joy. For Jesus also
assured us, "Peace I leave with you; my peace I give to

you; not as the world gives do I give to you. Let not your hearts be troubled, neither let them be afraid" (Jn 14:27). This was emphasized by St. Pius of Pietrelcina ("Padre Pio") in his suffering:

> You should be encouraged and comforted by the knowledge that we are not alone in our sufferings, for all the followers of the Nazarene scattered throughout the world suffer in the same manner. . . . Let us remember that the lot of chosen souls is to suffer. God, the author of all grace and of every gift leading to salvation, has decreed that glory will be ours on condition that we endure suffering with a Christian spirit. So let us lift up our hearts full of confidence in God alone. Let us humble ourselves beneath his powerful hand, let us cheerfully accept the trials to which the mercy of the heavenly Father subjects us, so that he may raise us up at the time of his visitation. Let all our concern be to love God and be pleasing to him, paying no attention to all the rest, in the knowledge that God will always take more care of us than we can say or imagine.[98]

As such, it helps if we understand that suffering provides a special opportunity to grow closer to Jesus and experience his peace, even in the midst of pain. Isn't it heartening to know that we can grow closer to Jesus in prayer, in Sacred Scripture, in unity with other Christians, and in the sacraments of confession and the Eucharist, especially when we are suffering?

We can grow closer to Jesus Christ and each other most effectively in and through the Church. The Church is a hospital for the wounded, not a haven for saints. Its doors opened two thousand years ago, and they are still open today. Inside these doors can be found true peace and joy, especially for those who are hopeless, hurting, or suffering.[99]

SUMMARY AND CONCLUSION

In this book, we have explored some possible answers to the big question, "Why would a loving God allow evil, pain, and suffering?" To be very clear, God does not want us to suffer and does not directly cause our suffering. This is crucial to understand. And it is very important to realize that one reason God permits us to experience pain, disease, tragedy, disappointment, and failure is because God is able to bring about a greater good out of any and all situations. That good may impact the sufferer, those who observe the sufferer, the Church, and the world in general—all to bring about a closer relationship to God for the salvation of mankind.

In part I of this book, we explored the question of why does a loving God allow disease and natural disasters. Natural or physical evil include events such as hurricanes and earthquakes, illnesses such as cancer and Alzheimer's, and disabilities such as blindness and deafness.

Most of us tend to put God in a tight little box during our good times, relegating him to Sunday morning (if we take the time for even that) and not giving God much of a thought during the rest of the week. And then when something bad happens, we blame God. However, diffi-culties and hardships can be blessings in disguise because they can be a catalyst and the means by which we become motivated to finally give ourselves to God and to seek his will in our lives. Suffering reminds us that we need to focus our lives on God and trust God in all things.

C. S. Lewis suggests pain and suffering are "God's megaphone to rouse a deaf world." As a wake-up call, suffering may re-orient us on the path God wants us to choose, and it may become a catalyst for others to choose that same path leading to ours and others' eternal salva-tion. Notice that God is not forcing us on the path to him through our suffering. God is merely allowing suffering so we can put our faith and trust in his unconditional love for us and choose God instead of the things of this world. From the beginning, we have been instructed, "You shall love the LORD your God with all your heart, and with all your soul, and with all your might" (Dt 6:5). We read in the testimonies of Marjoe and Jean Siongco, Martha Madri, and Bob Kaput how suffering helped them do this in their lives.

In part II, we explored the question of why a loving God allows evil human behavior (moral evil). Moral evil includes specific acts of intentional wrongdoing, such as lying, stealing, raping, and murdering. In brief, moral evil occurs because of misuse of the gift of our free will.

Mankind was created and given the gift of free will since humans are created in the image and likeness of God. This awesome gift can also be a terrible burden. Adam and Eve did not choose wisely, as their disobedi-ence—driven by their pride—wounded human nature and introduced evil, suffering, and death into the world. St. Thomas Aquinas identified four wounds to our human nature—namely, ignorance, malice, weakness, and concupiscence. These wounds are the fundamental reason for the suffering and moral evil in the world.

Suffering is an inevitable part of our fallen world. In our fallen human nature, the body tends inexorably towards death and the sufferings that foretell it. Everyone suffers. How we respond to suffering makes all the difference, as we saw in the testimonies of Richard McLeon, Aneel Aranha, and Terri Thomas.

In part III, we explored God's purposes for our life on earth. A primary purpose of our life on earth is to allow the grace of God to help us grow in personal virtue and goodness—to become more like Christ. Personal virtue is the mark of a life well lived, and it takes a lifetime to cultivate. All Christians, of whatever age, are called to seek the holiness and virtue that only God provides, often through suffering.

We do not become holy overnight; it's a lifelong process of allowing the power and presence of the Holy Spirit to remove our faults and shortcomings so that we can become perfect as our heavenly Father is perfect. For many people, this growth in holiness and virtue seems to occur most often during the hard times in our lives, the times of struggle, pain, and suffering.

Another primary purpose of our life on earth is to lovingly serve God and others. We serve God and others by lovingly giving of our time, talents, and treasure. Remember, Jesus said, "Truly, I say to you, as you did it

to one of the least of these my brethren, you did it to me"
(Mt 25:40).

Suffering can help us achieve these purposes in life
by transforming us from ego-centric orientation to a
God-centric orientation in at least the following ways:

1. Suffering can be a wake-up call to start the
   process to transform us from a superficial
   purpose and identity to a God-like purpose
   and identity.
2. It can re-ignite our growth in faith and
   deepen our trust in God.
3. It can cause us to rely more on others for
   assistance, which provides opportunities for
   others to serve.
4. It can help us further develop natural virtues
   (e.g., endurance, courage, fortitude, pru-
   dence, rationality, and temperance).
5. It can enable us to deepen our love by
   increasing our empathy, humility, forgiveness, and compassion.
6. It can enable us to "offer up" our suffering
   for others and help build God's Kingdom on
   earth by bringing inspiration and hope to
   the world.[100]

It seems as though the more we allow suffering to
transform us, the more we become in the image and likeness of God. So, in a resounding yes, suffering is important to our personal and spiritual growth and in focusing
our lives on lovingly serving God and others.

In part III, we also learned how prayerfully applying the conformity, conversion, confirmation, consistency, and conviction tests can help us discern what God wants us to do in any situation, including during difficult times, and how this helps us focus our lives on serving God and others. We also explored how suffering provides a special opportunity to grow closer to Jesus and experience his peace, even in the midst of pain and suffering. With this knowledge, we can confidently venture forth in faith and step out in courage, knowing that God's grace is sufficient for any situation we may face in life.

In summary, let's again read from the *Catechism of the Catholic Church*:

> If God the Father almighty, the Creator of the ordered and good world, cares for all his creatures, why does evil exist? To this question, as pressing as it is unavoidable and as painful as it is mysterious, no quick answer will suffice. Only Christian faith as a whole constitutes the answer to this question: the goodness of creation, the drama of sin and the patient love of God who comes to meet man by his covenants, the redemptive Incarnation of his Son, his gift of the Spirit, his gathering of the Church, the power of the sacraments and his call to a blessed life to which free creatures are invited to consent in advance, but from which, by a terrible mystery, they can also turn away in advance. There is not a single aspect of the Christian message that is not in part an answer to the question of evil. (309)

Conclusion

This earthly life is filled with great joy and great suffering. We are all on this journey, which can sometimes seem unbearable. No one wants to experience hardship, but we can trust that God is always there with us. We can take comfort and find strength knowing that, even when the world does not make sense, we do not have to walk alone through life. God is with us, loves each of us, and is truly in control.

God loves us eternally, but this does not mean we will not suffer greatly, some more than others, while here on earth. But even when we do not understand why bad things happen to good people, we can trust that God will work out all things for the good of those who love God. As St. Paul wrote, "We know that in everything God works for good with those who love him, who are called according to his purpose" (Rom 8:28) and "I consider that the sufferings of this present time are not worth comparing with the glory that is to be revealed to us" (Rom 8:18).

We should keep in mind that our trials and hardships will come to an end. They surely will. We all have times when we want to give up. But we know that God is present in the midst of our troubles and offers us the strength to persevere for our own good.

We need to let God shape our perspective during the difficult times. If we focus on trying to escape the pain and our trials, we may miss God's blessings. When we have patience and trust in God's care, we are able to look back on our past trials with thanksgiving and appreciation for the good they brought us.

God truly does love and care for each of us. Even the sufferings and hardships in our lives are signs of God's love and special opportunities for spiritual growth if we turn to God and place our hope and trust in him. We are called to embrace our cross and trust in the God who loves us eternally.

God also calls upon us to share in the sufferings of others. Simply put, we are to bear the burdens of one another, just as Christ carried our burdens on the cross. We are to be "Christ with skin on" for one another.

May we always see the trials and difficulties of this life as opportunities to help others, to grow closer to Jesus, to grow in our faith and trust in God, and to grow in personal holiness. For the most difficult paths in life are the ones that often lead to the most beautiful views. May this understanding give us patience, hope, and peace as we and those we love face life's inevitable trials and troubles.

BIBLIOGRAPHY

Kreeft, Peter and Ronald K. Tacelli, *Handbook of Catholic Apologetics: Reasoned Answers to Questions of Faith* (San Francisco: Ignatius Press, 2009)

Kreeft, Peter, *Making Sense Out of Suffering* (Cincinnati, Ohio: St. Anthony Messenger, 1986)

Lewis, C. S., *The Problem of Pain* (New York: HarperCollins Publishers, 2001)

Scanlan, Michael, with Jim Manney, *The Truth About Trouble: How Hard Times Can Draw You Closer to God* (Cincinnati, Ohio: Servant Books, 2005)

Scanlan, Michael, *What Does God Want? A Practical Guide to Making Decisions* (Huntington, Indiana: Our Sunday Visitor Publishing Division, 1996)

Schuchts, Bob, *Real Suffering: Finding Hope and Healing in the Trials of Life* (Charlotte, North Carolina: Saint Benedict Press, 2018)

Shaw, Russell, *Does Suffering Make Sense?* (Princeton, New Jersey: Scepter Publishers, 2000)

Spitzer, Robert, *The Light Shines On in the Darkness: Transforming Suffering through Faith* (San Francisco: Ignatius Press, 2017)

Warren, Rick, *The Purpose Driven Life: What On Earth Am I Here For?* (Grand Rapids, Michigan: Zondervan, 2002)

APPENDIX OF BIBLE ABBREVIATIONS

Bible Book Names and Their Abbreviations

Old Testament

Genesis	Gn	Esther	Est
Exodus	Ex	Job	Jb
Leviticus	Lv	Psalms	Ps
Numbers	Nm	Proverbs	Prv
Deuteronomy	Dt	Ecclesiastes	Eccl
Joshua	Jo	Song of Songs	Sg
Judges	Jgs	Wisdom of	
Ruth	Ru	Solomon	Ws
1 Samuel	1 Sm	Sirach	Sir
2 Samuel	2 Sm	Isaiah	Is
1 Kings	1 Kgs	Jeremiah	Jer
2 Kings	2 Kgs	Lamentations	Lam
1 Chronicles	1 Chr	Baruch	Bar
2 Chronicles	2 Chr	Ezekiel	Ez
Ezra	Ezr	Daniel	Dn
Nehemiah	Neh	Hosea	Hos
Tobit	Tb	Joel	Jl
Judith	Jdt	Amos	Am

Obadiah . . . . .Ob
Jonah . . . . .Jon
Micah . . . . .Mi
Nahum . . . . .Na
Habakkuk . . . . . . .Hb
Zephaniah . . . . . . .Zep

Haggai . . . . .Hg
Zechariah. . . . . . . .Zec
Malachi . . . . .Mal
1 Maccabees . . . . .1 Mc
2 Maccabees . . . . .2 Mc

New Testament
St. Matthew . . . . . .Mt
St. Mark . . . . .Mk
St. Luke. . . . . .Lk
St. John. . . . . .Jn
Acts of the
    Apostles . . . . . . .Acts
Romans . . . . .Rom
1 Corinthians . . . .1 Cor
2 Corinthians . . . .2 Cor
Galatians . . . . .Gal
Ephesians. . . . . . . .Eph
Philippians. . . . . . .Phil
Colossians . . . . . . .Col
1 Thessalonians. . .1 Thes

2 Thessalonians. . .2 Thes
1 Timothy . . . . . . .1 Tm
2 Timothy . . . . . . .2 Tm
Titus . . . . .Ti
Philemon . . . . .Phlm
Hebrews. . . . . .Heb
St. James. . . . . .Jas
1 St. Peter. . . . . . . .1 Pt
2 St. Peter. . . . . . . .2 Pt
1 St. John . . . . .1 Jn
2 St. John . . . . .2 Jn
3 St. John . . . . .3 Jn
St. Jude . . . . .Jude
Revelation . . . . . . .Rv

NOTES

1   "Ten Life-Transforming Truths," Magis Center, July 27, 2010, https://www.magiscenter.com/ten-life-transforming-truths/.

2   C. S. Lewis, *The Problem of Pain* (New York: HarperCollins Publishers, 2001), p. 94.

3   John Stonestreet, "Happy Lent. Seriously." Breakpoint, March 6, 2019, https://www.breakpoint.org/happy-lent-seriously-2/.

4   C. S. Lewis, *The Problem of Pain*, p. 91.

5   Pope Francis, "Pope Francis' Urbi et Orbi address on coronavirus and Jesus calming the storm," *America*, March 27, 2020, https://www.americamagazine.org/faith/2020/03/27/read-pope-francis-urbi-et-orbi-address-coronavirus-and-jesus-calming-storm.

6   See http://www.jesusfactorfiction.com/lifestories/randall.html.

7   C. S. Lewis, *The Problem of Pain*, p. 88.

8   Rick Warren, *The Purpose Driven Life: What On Earth Am I Here For?* (Grand Rapids, Michigan: Zondervan, 2002), p. 194.

9   Bill McGarvey, "In Defense of Suffering," *America*, September 26, 2016, https://www.americamagazine.org/issue/help-your-brothers.

10   Pope John Paul II, apostolic letter *Salvifici Doloris: On the Christian Meaning of Human Suffering*, 1984, https://w2.vatican.va/content/john-paul-ii/en/apost_letters/1984/documents/hf_jp-ii_apl_11021984_salvifici-doloris.html (#26).

11   Renzo Allegri, "St. Francis' Conversion," *Messenger of Saint Anthony*, September 22, 2006, http://www.messengersaintanthony.com/content/st-francis-conversion.

12   Wikipedia, s.v. "Ignatius of Loyola," last modified December 5, 2020, 20:40, https://en.wikipedia.org/wiki/Ignatius_of_Loyola#Religious_conversion_and_visions.

13   Wikipedia, s.v. "Joni Eareckson Tada," last modified November 11, 2020, http://en.wikipedia.org/wiki/Joni_Eareckson_Tada.

14   Quoted in: *The Case for Faith* DVD (La Mirada, California: La Mirada Films, 2008).

15   John Stonestreet, "Fifty years ago, Joni Eareckson Tada's life changed forever. And since then, God has used her transform the lives of countless others," Breakpoint, August 11, 2017, https://mailchi.mp/colsoncenter/email-subject-line-17497.

16   "St. Rose of Lima," Crossroads Initiative, August 23, 2016, https://www.crossroadsinitiative.com/media/articles/rose-lima-grace-august-23/.

17   Thomas a Kempis, *The Imitation of Christ: With Reflections From the Documents of Vatican II for*

Each Chapter (Homebush, New South Wales, Australia: St. Paul Publications, 1992), Book I, Chapter 22, p. 79; Book II, Chapter 8, p. 121 and Chapter 12, p. 135.

18 "Ten Life-Transforming Truths," Magis Center, July 27, 2010, https://www.magiscenter.com/ten-life-transforming-truths/.

19 See http://www.tertullian.org/fathers/augustine_enchiridion_02_trans.htm#C8 (#27).

20 Charles Johnston, "Question; Offering up Suffering," *Now That I'm Catholic* (blog), https://nowthatimcatholic.wordpress.com/2017/07/10/question-offering-up-suffering/.

21 *YOUCAT: Youth Catechism of the Catholic Church* (San Francisco: Ignatius Press, 2011), p. 67.

22 Paul D. Scalia, "Three Lessons from Lourdes," *The Catholic Thing*, February 11, 2017, https://www.thecatholicthing.org/2017/02/11/three-lessons-from-lourdes/.

23 See https://w2.vatican.va/content/john-paul-ii/en/apost_letters/1984/documents/hf_jp-ii_apl_11021984_salvifici-doloris.html (#19).

24 Charles Pope, "What is Lacking in Christ's passion?" Our Sunday Visitor, January 20, 2020, https://www.osvnews.com/2020/01/20/what-is-lacking-in-christs-passion/.

25 Pete Socks, "CBB Interview with Julie Onderko," *The Catholic Book Blogger*, June 21, 2016, http://www.patheos.com/blogs/catholicbookblogger/2016/06/21/cbb-interview-with-julie-onderko/.

26 "Daily Quote from St. John of the Cross," Integrated Catholic Life, October 29, 2011, http://www.integratedcatholiclife.org/2011/10/daily-quote-from-st-john-of-the-cross-8/.

27 See "What About Natural Evil?" *Reasonable Faith*, July 19, 2011, https://www.reasonablefaith.org/media/reasonable-faith-podcast/what-about-natural-evil.

28 Ibid.

29 Steven R. Hemler, *The Reality of God: The Layman's Guide to Scientific Evidence for the Creator* (Charlotte, North Carolina: St. Benedict Press, 2014), p. 46.

30 See "What About Natural Evil?" *Reasonable Faith*, July 19, 2011, https://www.reasonablefaith.org/media/reasonable-faith-podcast/what-about-natural-evil.

31 Robert Barron, "Jackie and the Priest," Catholic World Report, April 4, 2017, http://www.catholicworldreport.com/2017/04/04/jackie-and-the-priest/.

32 See John Stonestreet, "Fifty years ago, Joni Eareckson Tada's life changed forever. And since then, God has used her transform the lives of countless others," Breakpoint, August 11, 2017, https://mailchi.mp/colsoncenter/email-subject-line-17497.

33 C. S. Lewis, *The Problem of Pain*, p. 63.

34 See Carol D'Souza, "On Four Wounds Due to Original Sin – St. Thomas Aquinas," Chosen to Be Catholic, December 5, 2016, https://catholicprayersonline.wordpress.com/2016/12/05/on-four-wounds-due-to-original-sin-st-thomas-aquinas/.

35   Glenn M. Spencer, "The Four Wounds of the Fall,"
      All Saints Anglican Church, January 21, 2016,
      http://www.allsaintscville.org/the-four-wounds-
      of-the-fall/.

36   Walter Farrell and Martin J. Healy, *My Way of Life:
      The Summa Simplified for Everyone* (Brooklyn:
      New York, Confraternity of the Precious Blood,
      1952), pp. 283–84.

37   Charles Pope, "The Problem of Polygenism in
      Accepting the Theory of Evolution," *Community
      on Mission* (blog), October 18, 2010, http://blog.
      adw.org/2010/10/polygenism/.

38   Tim Staples, "Were Adam and Eve Real or Sym-
      bols?" Tim Staples (blog), http://www.timstaples.
      com//blog/were-adam-and-eve-real-or-symbols.

39   John Paul II, "Humans Are Spiritual and Corpo-
      real Beings," Inters, April 16, 1986, http://inters.
      org/John-Paul-II-Catechesis-Spiritual-Corporeal.

40   Steven Hemler, *The Reality of God*, p. 91.

41   Peter Kreeft and Ronald K. Tacelli, *Handbook of
      Catholic Apologetics*, pp. 143–44.

42   See Daniel Doctor, "NO to Hell, Satan& Sin,"
      Mother of God (forum discussion), October 28,
      2017, http://motheofgod.com/threads/no-to-hell-
      satan-sin.11350/.

43   See Pope Francis, apostolic exhortation *Guadete
      Et Exsultate* (March 2018), http://w2.vatican.va/
      content/francesco/en/apost_exhortations/docu-
      ments/papa-francesco_esortazione-ap_20180319_
      gaudete-et-exsultate.html#More_than_a_myth.

44   "Ten Life-Transforming Truths," Magis Center,
      July 27, 2010, https://www.magiscenter.com/ten-
      life-transforming-truths/.

45   C. S. Lewis, *Mere Christianity* (New York: Harper-Collins Publishers, 2001), p. 50.

46   "Ten Life-Transforming Truths," Magis Center, July 27, 2010, https://www.magiscenter.com/ten-life-transforming-truths/.

47   C. S. Lewis, *The Problem of Pain*, p. 70.

48   Dwight Longenecker, "Why Does God Allow Horrible Evil?" National Catholic Register, February 23, 2017, http://www.ncregister.com/blog/longenecker/why-does-god-allow-horrible-evil.

49   Robert Spitzer, "Why Does God Allow Suffering?" December 6, 2020, https://blog.magiscenter.com/blog/why-does-god-allow-suffering.

50   "The Command—and Capacity—to Love," Daily Meditation with Magnificat, https://aleteia.org/daily-prayer/sunday-october-25/daily-meditation-1/.

51   See http://www.catholic-forum.com/themes/st_anslem.html.

52   Benedict XVI, general audience, January 12, 2011, http://w2.vatican.va/content/benedict-xvi/en/audiences/2011/documents/hf_ben-xvi_aud_20110112.html.

53   For example, see Alice Miller, "Childhood: The Unexplored Source of Knowledge," The Natural Child Project, http://www.naturalchild.org/alice_miller/childhood.html.

54   John Powell, *Why Am I Afraid to Tell You Who I Am? Insights into Personal Growth* (Allen, Texas: Thomas More Publishing, 1998), p. 117.

55   See https://staugny.org/quotes.

56 See http://dailyscripture.servantsoftheword.org/readings/2016/may13.htm.

57 *The Upper Room: Where the World Meets to Pray*, March-April 2017, p. 70.

58 Rick Warren, *The Purpose Driven Life*, p. 235.

59 See Paul D. Scalia, "Three Lessons from Lourdes," *The Catholic Thing*, February 11, 2017, https://www.thecatholicthing.org/2017/02/11/three-lessons-from-lourdes/.

60 Steven R. Hemler, *Search No More: The Keys to Truth and Happiness* (Charlotte, North Carolina: TAN Books, 2019), Part 3.

61 *Catechism of the Catholic Church*, p. 116, paragraph 460.

62 Pope Francis, apostolic exhortation *Guadete Et Exsultate* (March 2018), See http://w2.vatican.va/content/francesco/en/apost_exhortations/documents/papa-francesco_esortazione-ap_20180319_gaudete-et-exsultate.html (#14 & 15).

63 Rick Warren, *The Purpose Driven Life*, p. 193.

64 Michael Scanlan, *What Does God Want? A Practical Guide to Making Decisions* (Huntington, Indiana: Our Sunday Visitor Publishing Division, 1996), pp. 111–12.

65 See Homily of John Paul II, *Canonization of St. Pio of Pietrelcina*, http://www.vatican.va/content/john-paul-ii/en/homilies/2002/documents/hf_jp-ii_hom_20020616_padre-pio.html.

66 See John Paul II, apostolic letter *Salvifici Doloris* (1984), https://w2.vatican.va/content/john-paul-ii/en/apost_letters/1984/documents/hf_jp-ii_apl_11021984_salvifici-doloris.html (#12 & 27).

67   Rick Warren, *The Purpose Driven Life*, p. 197.

68   See https://www.crossroadsinitiative.com/media/
articles/thecrossexemplifieseveryvirtue/.

69   See John Paul II, apostolic letter *Salvifici Doloris*
(1984), https://w2.vatican.va/content/john-paul-ii/
en/apost_letters/1984/documents/hf_jp-ii_
apl_11021984_salvifici-doloris.html (#21).

70   John of the Cross, "A Spiritual Canticle of St John
of the Cross: Recognizing the mystery hidden
within Christ Jesus," http://ldysinger.stjohnsem.
edu/@texts2/1585_jn_cross/02_john-txt1.htm.

71   Karlo Broussard, *Purgatory Is For Real: Good News
About the Afterlife for Those Who Aren't Perfect
Yet* (El Cajon, California: Catholic Answers Press,
2020), pp. 113-148.

72   See D. D. Emmons, "Purgatory according to St.
Catherine of Genoa," *Our Sunday Visitor*, June 20,
2019, https://www.osvnews.com/2019/06/20/pur-
gatory-according-to-st-catherine-of-genoa/.

73   Ibid.

74   *Handbook for Today's Catholic* (Liguori, Missouri:
Liguori Publications, 1994), pp. 47–48.

75   *YOUCAT: Youth Catechism of the Catholic Church*,
p. 96.

76   Rick Warren, *The Purpose Driven Life*, p. 232.

77   Rick Warren, *The Purpose Driven Life*, pp. 246–47.

78   See http://www.catholicity.com/prayer/prayers-
and-hymns-by-john-henry-cardinal-newman.
html.

79   See https://www.goodreads.com/author/
quotes/30796.Hans_Urs_von_Balthasar.

80   Edgar Albert Guest, *The Path to Home* (Chicago: The Reilly & Lee Company, 1919), p. 36.

81   Michael Scanlan, *What Does God Want? A Practical Guide to Making Decisions* (Huntington, Indiana: Our Sunday Visitor Publishing Division, 1996).

82   Michael Scanlan, *What Does God Want?*, p. 48.

83   Michael Scanlan, *What Does God Want?*, p. 15.

84   Michael Scanlan, *What Does God Want?*, p. 27.

85   Michael Scanlan, *What Does God Want?*, pp. 55, 63.

86   Michael Scanlan, *What Does God Want?*, p. 40.

87   See Steven R. Hemler, "An Abortion Public Policy Proposal," https://hsiweb.org/index.php/articles/ steve-hemler/life-s-little -learnings/item/385-an-abortion-public-policy -proposal.

88   "Terry, Allen Launch Attacks in Debate," *Daily Press: Hampton Roads' Newspaper*, July 11, 1993, p. 1.

89   Steven R. Hemler, Richard G. Wilkins, and Frank H. Fischer, "Abortion: A Principled Politics," *National Review*, December 27, 1993, pp. 40-41.

90   Steven R. Hemler, Richard G. Wilkins, and Frank H. Fischer, "Abortion: A Principled Politics," *The Human Life Review*, Winter 1994, pp. 101-103.

91   Michael Scanlan, *What Does God Want?*, p. 71.

92   Peter Kreeft, *Making Sense Out of Suffering* (Cincinnati, Ohio: St. Anthony Messenger, 1986), p. 129.

93   See https://www.goodreads.com/quotes/216250-pain-and-suffering-have-come-into-your-life-but-remember.

94   See Kevin C. Rhoades, "The Meaning and Value of Suffering," *Today's Catholic*, November 8, 2017, https://todayscatholic.org/meaning-value-suffering/.

95   Brandon Vogt, *Return: How to Draw Your Child Back to the Church* (Winter Springs, Florida: Numinous Books, 2015), p. 221.

96   See Pope Francis, "Read: Pope Francis' Urbi et Orbi address on coronavirus and Jesus calming the storm," *America*, March 27, 2020, https://www.americamagazine.org/faith/2020/03/27/read-pope-francis-urbi-et-orbi-address-coronavirus-and-jesus-calming-storm.

97   *The Word Among Us*, January 2019 (Volume 38, Number 2), p. 29.

98   Padre Pio of Pietrelcina, *Letters, Volume II: Correspondence with Raffaelina Cerase, Noblewoman (1914-1915)*, Mary F. Ingoldsby, Tr. (San Giovanni Rotondo, Italy: Our Lady of Grace Friary, 1997).

99   See Matthew Becklo, "The suicide epidemic and a message for a hopeless world," *Aleteia*, June 8, 2018, https://aleteia.org/2018/06/08/the-suicide-epidemic-and-a-message-for-a-hopeless-world/.

100   Robert Spitzer, *The Light Shines On in the Darkness: Transforming Suffering through Faith* (San Francisco: Ignatius Press, 2017), pp. 71-72.

ABOUT THE AUTHOR

Steven Hemler is president of the Catholic Apologetics Institute of North America (see www.cainaweb.org). He is also author of *The Reality of God: The Layman's Guide to Scientific Evidence for the Creator* and *Search No More: The Keys to Truth and Happiness*, both published by St. Benedict Press and TAN Books.